The Federal Reserve System

Purposes & Functions

First Edition, May 1939

Second Edition, November 1947

Third Edition, April 1954

Fourth Edition, February 1961

Fifth Edition, December 1963

Sixth Edition, September 1974

Seventh Edition, December 1984

Eighth Edition, December 1994

Ninth Edition, June 2005

Tenth Edition, October 2016

Publications Fulfillment

(e-mail) Publications-BOG@frb.gov

(ph) 202-452-3245

(fax) 202-728-5886

(mail) Mail Stop N-127

Board of Governors of the Federal Reserve System

20th Street and Constitution Avenue NW

Washington, DC 20551

Contents

Overview of the Federal Reserve System

The Federal Reserve performs five key functions in the public interest to promote the health of the U.S. economy and the stability of the U.S. financial system.

1

$\mathcal{T}$he Federal Reserve System is the central bank of the United States. It performs five general functions to promote the effective operation of the U.S. economy and, more generally, the public interest. The Federal Reserve

- **conducts the nation's monetary policy** to promote maximum employment, stable prices, and moderate long-term interest rates in the U.S. economy;

- **promotes the stability of the financial system** and seeks to minimize and contain systemic risks through active monitoring and engagement in the U.S. and abroad;

- **promotes the safety and soundness of individual financial institutions** and monitors their impact on the financial system as a whole;

Figure 1.1. The Federal Reserve System

The Federal Reserve is unique among central banks. By statute, Congress provided for a central banking system with public and private characteristics. The System performs five functions in the public interest.

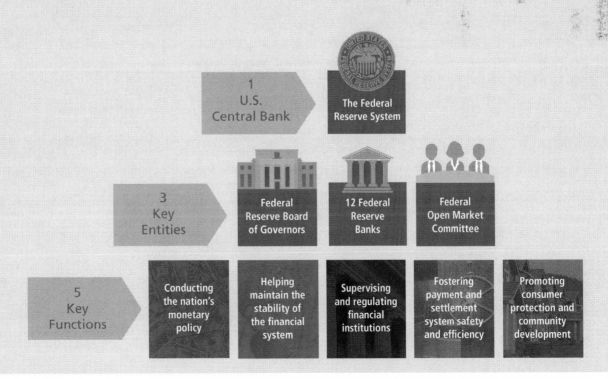

- **fosters payment and settlement system safety and efficiency** through services to the banking industry and the U.S. government that facilitate U.S.-dollar transactions and payments; and

- **promotes consumer protection and community development** through consumer-focused supervision and examination, research and analysis of emerging consumer issues and trends, community economic development activities, and the administration of consumer laws and regulations.

The Federal Reserve was established to serve the public interest.

. . . .

The U.S. Approach to Central Banking

The framers of the Federal Reserve Act purposely rejected the concept of a single central bank. Instead, they provided for a central banking "system" with three salient features: (1) a central governing Board, (2) a decentralized operating structure of 12 Reserve Banks, and (3) a combination of public and private characteristics.

Although parts of the Federal Reserve System share some characteristics with private-sector entities, the Federal Reserve was established to serve the public interest.

There are three key entities in the Federal Reserve System: the Board of Governors, the Federal Reserve Banks (Reserve Banks), and the Federal Open Market Committee (FOMC). The Board of Governors, an agency of the federal government that reports to and is directly accountable to Congress (figure 1.2), provides general guidance for the System and oversees the 12 Reserve Banks.

Figure 1.2. Three key entities, serving the public interest

The framers of the Federal Reserve Act developed a central banking system that would broadly represent the public interest.

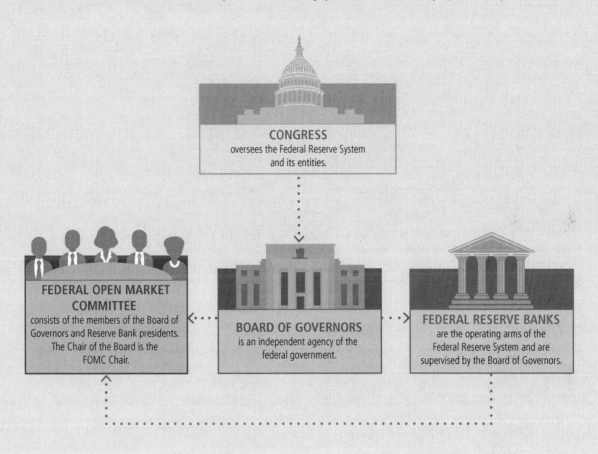

Within the System, certain responsibilities are shared between the Board of Governors in Washington, D.C., whose members are appointed by the President with the advice and consent of the Senate, and the Federal Reserve Banks and Branches, which constitute the System's operating presence around the country. While the Federal Reserve has frequent communication with executive branch and congressional officials, its decisions are made independently.

The Decentralized System
Structure and Its Philosophy

In establishing the Federal Reserve System, the United States was divided geographically into 12 Districts, each with a separately incorporated Reserve Bank. District boundaries were based on prevailing trade regions that existed in 1913 and related economic considerations, so they do not necessarily coincide with state lines (figure 1.3).

As originally envisioned, each of the 12 Reserve Banks was intended to operate independently from the other Reserve Banks. Variation was expected in discount rates—the interest rate that commercial banks

Figure 1.3. Twelve Federal Reserve Districts operate independently but with supervision

Federal Reserve District boundaries are based on economic considerations; the Districts operate independently but under the supervision of the Federal Reserve Board of Governors.

were charged for borrowing funds from a Reserve Bank. The setting of a separately determined discount rate appropriate to each District was considered the most important tool of monetary policy at that time. The concept of national economic policymaking was not well developed, and the impact of open market operations—purchases and sales of U.S. government securities—on policymaking was less significant.

Revisions to the Federal Reserve Act in 1933 and 1935 created the modern-day Federal Open Market Committee.

As the nation's economy became more integrated and more complex, through advances in technology, communications, transportation, and financial services, the effective conduct of monetary policy began to require increased collaboration and coordination throughout the System. This was accomplished in part through revisions to the Federal Reserve Act in 1933 and 1935 that together created the modern-day FOMC.

The Depository Institutions Deregulation and Monetary Control Act of 1980 (Monetary Control Act) introduced an even greater degree of coordination among Reserve Banks with respect to the pricing of financial services offered to depository institutions. There has also been a trend among Reserve Banks to centralize or consolidate many of their financial services and support functions and to standardize others. Reserve Banks have become more efficient by entering into intra-System service agreements that allocate responsibilities for services and functions that are national in scope among each of the 12 Reserve Banks.

The Reserve Banks: A Blend of Private and Governmental Characteristics

Pursuant to the Federal Reserve Act, each of the 12 Reserve Banks is separately incorporated and has a nine-member board of directors.

Commercial banks that are members of the Federal Reserve System hold stock in their District's Reserve Bank and elect six of the Reserve Bank's directors; three remaining directors are appointed by the Board of Governors. Most Reserve Banks have at least one Branch, and each Branch has its own board of directors. Branch directors are appointed by either the Reserve Bank or the Board of Governors.

Directors serve as a link between the Federal Reserve and the private sector. As a group, directors bring to their duties a wide variety of experiences in the private sector, which gives them invaluable insight into the economic conditions of their respective Federal Reserve Districts. Reserve Bank head-office and Branch directors contribute to the System's overall understanding of the economy.

The Federal Reserve is not funded by congressional appropriations. Its operations are financed primarily from the interest earned on the securities it owns—securities acquired in the course of the Federal Reserve's open market operations. The fees received for priced services provided to depository institutions—such as check clearing, funds transfers, and automated clearinghouse operations—are another source of income; this income is used to cover the cost of those services. After payment of expenses and transfers to surplus (limited to an aggregate of $10 billion), all the net earnings of the Federal Reserve Banks are transferred to the U.S. Treasury (figure 1.4).

Is Reserve Bank stock like regular corporate stock?

The 12 regional Federal Reserve Banks issue shares of stock to member banks. Owning Reserve Bank stock is, however, quite different from owning stock in a private company. The Reserve Banks are not operated for profit, and ownership of a certain amount of stock is, by law, a condition of membership in the System. The stock may not be sold, traded, or pledged as security for a loan, and dividends are, by law, paid to member banks at a maximum rate of 6 percent, determined in part by each member bank's total assets.

Despite the need for coordination and consistency throughout the Federal Reserve System, geographic distinctions remain important. Effective monetary policymaking requires knowledge and input about regional differences. For example, two directors from the same industry may have different opinions regarding the strength or weakness of that sector, depending on their regional perspectives. The decentralized structure of the System and its blend of private and public characteristics, envisioned by the System's creators, therefore, remain important features today.

Figure 1.4. Federal Reserve net earnings are paid to the U.S. Treasury

The Federal Reserve transfers its net earnings to the U.S. Treasury.

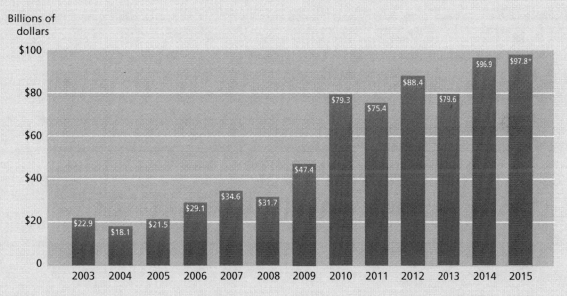

* Does not include $19.3 billion also transferred to the U.S. Treasury from Reserve Bank capital surplus per the Fixing America's Surface Transportation Act.

Source: Federal Reserve Board news release, January 10, 2013 (available in the News & Events section of the Federal Reserve Board's website, www.federalreserve.gov).

The Three Key System Entities

The Board of Governors, the Federal Reserve Banks, and the Federal Open Market Committee work together to promote the health of the U.S. economy and the stability of the U.S. financial system.

2

$\mathscr{T}$hree key Federal Reserve entities—the Federal Reserve Board of Governors (Board of Governors), the Federal Reserve Banks (Reserve Banks), and the Federal Open Market Committee (FOMC)—make decisions that help promote the health of the U.S. economy and the stability of the U.S. financial system.

Figure 2.1. How the Federal Reserve operates within the U.S. government framework

A statutory framework established by the U.S. Congress guides the operation of the Federal Reserve System.

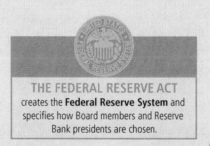

THE FEDERAL RESERVE ACT
creates the **Federal Reserve System** and specifies how Board members and Reserve Bank presidents are chosen.

PRESIDENT
nominates members of the **Board of Governors**, the chief governing body of the Federal Reserve System, and nominates one Board member to be Chair and one to be Vice Chair.

SENATE
confirms Board members appointed by the President to staggered 14-year terms, and confirms the nominations of Board members to be either Chair or Vice Chair.

BOARD OF GOVERNORS
Seven Board members guide all aspects of the operation of the Federal Reserve System and its five key functions.

FEDERAL RESERVE BANKS
12 Reserve Banks examine and supervise financial institutions, act as lenders of last resort, and provide U.S. payment system services, among other things.

FEDERAL OPEN MARKET COMMITTEE
Seven Board members and five Reserve Bank presidents direct open market operations that sets U.S. monetary policy to promote maximum employment, stable prices, and moderate long-term interest rates in the U.S. economy.

The Federal Reserve Board: Selection and Function

The Board of Governors—located in Washington, D.C.—is the governing body of the Federal Reserve System. It is run by seven members, or "governors," who are nominated by the President of the United States and confirmed in their positions by the U.S. Senate. The Board of Governors guides the operation of the Federal Reserve System to promote the goals and fulfill the responsibilities given to the Federal Reserve by the Federal Reserve Act.

All of the members of the Board serve on the FOMC, which is the body within the Federal Reserve that sets monetary policy (see "The Federal Open Market Committee: Selection and Function" on page 15). Each member of the Board of Governors is appointed for a 14-year term; the terms are staggered so that one term expires on January 31 of each even-numbered year. After serving a full 14-year term, a Board member may not be reappointed. If a Board member leaves the Board before his or her term expires, however, the person nominated and confirmed to serve the remainder of the term may later be appointed to a full 14-year term (figure 2.2).

The Chair and Vice Chair of the Board are also appointed by the President and confirmed by the Senate, but serve only four-year terms. They may be reappointed to additional four-year terms. The nominees to these posts must already be members of the Board or must be simultaneously appointed to the Board.

The Board oversees the operations of the 12 Reserve Banks and shares with them the responsibility for supervising and regulating certain financial institutions and activities (see section 5, "Supervising and Regulating Financial Institutions and Activities," on page 72). The Board also provides general guidance, direction, and oversight when the Reserve Banks lend to depository institutions and when the Reserve

Figure 2.2. Serving on the Board of Governors

The Federal Reserve's governors serve staggered 14-year terms and may not be reappointed; all governors—including the Chair and Vice Chair—are appointed by the President and confirmed by the Senate.

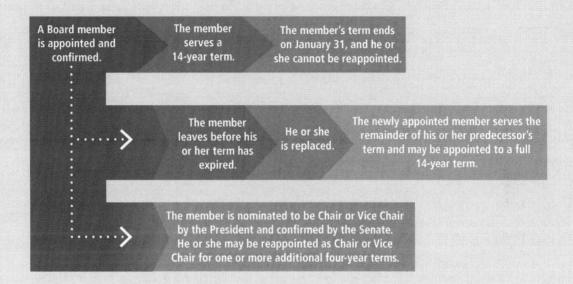

Banks provide financial services to depository institutions and the federal government. The Board also has broad oversight responsibility for the operations and activities of the Federal Reserve Banks (see section 6, "Fostering Payment and Settlement System Safety and Efficiency," on page 118). This authority includes oversight of the Reserve Banks' services to depository institutions, and to the U.S. Treasury, and of the Reserve Banks' examination and supervision of various financial institutions. As part of this oversight, the Board reviews and approves the budgets of each of the Reserve Banks.

The Board also helps to ensure that the voices and concerns of consumers and communities are heard at the central bank by conducting consumer-focused supervision, research, and policy analysis, and, more generally, by promoting a fair and transparent consumer financial services market (see section 7, "Promoting Consumer Protection and Community Development," on page 152).

The Federal Reserve Banks: Structure and Function

The 12 Federal Reserve Banks and their 24 Branches are the operating arms of the Federal Reserve System. Each Reserve Bank operates within its own particular geographic area, or district, of the United States.

Each Reserve Bank gathers data and other information about the businesses and the needs of local communities in its region. That information is then factored into monetary policy decisions by the FOMC and other decisions made by the Board of Governors.

Figure 2.3. Composition of Federal Reserve Bank boards of directors and selection of Reserve Bank presidents

The boards of directors of the Reserve Banks represent a cross-section of banking, commercial, agricultural, and industrial interests. Six of the nine members of each board of directors are chosen to represent the public interest; those six board directors nominate their Bank's president.

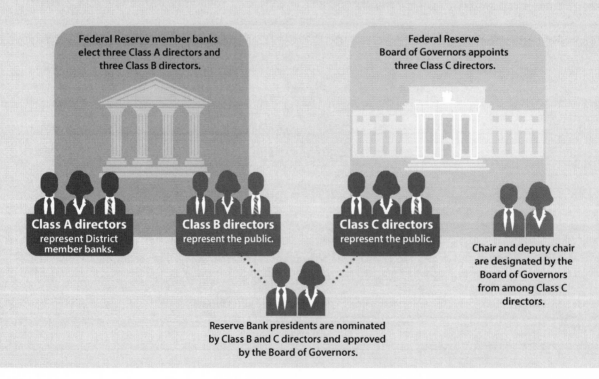

Federal Reserve member banks elect three Class A directors and three Class B directors.

Federal Reserve Board of Governors appoints three Class C directors.

Class A directors represent District member banks.

Class B directors represent the public.

Class C directors represent the public.

Chair and deputy chair are designated by the Board of Governors from among Class C directors.

Reserve Bank presidents are nominated by Class B and C directors and approved by the Board of Governors.

Reserve Bank Leadership

As set forth in the Federal Reserve Act, each Reserve Bank is subject to "the supervision and control of a board of directors." Much like the boards of directors of private corporations, Reserve Bank boards are responsible for overseeing their Bank's administration and governance, reviewing the Bank's budget and overall performance, overseeing the Bank's audit process, and developing broad strategic goals and directions. However, unlike private corporations, Reserve Banks are not operated in the interest of shareholders, but rather in the public interest.

Each year, the Board of Governors designates one chair and one deputy chair for each Reserve Bank board from among its Class C directors. The Federal Reserve Act requires that the chair of a Reserve Bank's board be a person of "tested banking experience," a term which has been interpreted as requiring familiarity with banking or financial services.

Each Reserve Bank board delegates responsibility for day-to-day operations to the president of that Reserve Bank and his or her staff. Reserve Bank presidents act as chief executive officers of their respective Banks and also serve, in rotation, as voting members of the FOMC. Presidents are nominated by a Bank's Class B and C directors and approved by the Board of Governors for five-year terms.

Reserve Bank Branches also have boards of directors. Pursuant to policy established by the Board of Governors, Branch boards must have either five or seven members. All Branch directors are appointed: the majority of directors on a Branch board are appointed by the Reserve Bank, and the remaining directors on the board are appointed by the Board of Governors. Each Branch board selects a chair from among those directors appointed by the Board of Governors. Unlike Reserve Bank directors, Branch directors are not divided into different classes. However, Branch directors must meet different eligibility requirements, depending on whether they are appointed by the Reserve Bank or the Board of Governors.

Want to learn more about Reserve Bank directors?

Reserve Bank and Branch directors play a number of roles at their Banks. To learn more about director responsibilities and requirements, see *Roles and Responsibilities of Federal Reserve Directors* in the About the Fed section of the Board's website, www.federalreserve.gov/aboutthefed/directors/about.htm.

Reserve Bank and Branch directors are elected or appointed for staggered three-year terms. When a director does not serve a full term, his or her successor is elected or appointed to serve the unexpired portion of that term.

Reserve Bank Responsibilities

The Reserve Banks carry out Federal Reserve core functions by

1. **supervising and examining state member banks** (state-chartered banks that have chosen to become members of the Federal Reserve System), bank and thrift holding companies, and nonbank financial institutions that have been designated as systemically important under authority delegated to them by the Board;

2. **lending to depository institutions** to ensure liquidity in the financial system;

3. **providing key financial services** that undergird the nation's payment system, including distributing the nation's currency and coin to depository institutions, clearing checks, operating the FedWire and automated clearinghouse (ACH) systems, and serving as a bank for the U.S. Treasury; and

4. **examining certain financial institutions** to ensure and enforce compliance with federal consumer protection and fair lending laws, while also promoting local community development.

In its role providing key financial services, the Reserve Bank acts, essentially, as a financial institution for the banks, thrifts, and credit unions in its District—that is, each Reserve Bank acts as a "bank for banks." In that capacity, it offers (and charges for) services to these depository institutions similar to those that ordinary banks provide their individual and business customers: the equivalent of checking accounts; loans; coin and currency; safekeeping services; and payment services (such as the processing of checks and the making of recurring and nonrecurring small- and large-dollar payments) that help banks, and ultimately their customers, buy and sell goods, services, and securities.

In addition, through their leaders and their connections to, and interactions with, members of their local communities, Federal Reserve Banks provide the Federal Reserve System with a wealth of information on conditions in virtually every part of the nation—information that is vital to formulating a national monetary policy that will help to maintain the health of the economy and the stability of the nation's financial system.

Certain information gathered by the Reserve Banks from Reserve Bank directors and other sources is also shared with the public prior to each FOMC meeting in a report commonly known as the Beige Book. In addition, every two weeks, the board of each Reserve Bank recommends discount rates (interest rates to be charged for loans to depository institutions made through that Bank's discount window); these interest rate recommendations are subject to review and determination by the Board of Governors.

The Federal Open Market Committee: Selection and Function

The FOMC is the body of the Federal Reserve System that sets national monetary policy (figure 2.4). The FOMC makes all decisions regarding the conduct of open market operations, which affect the federal funds rate (the rate at which depository institutions lend to each other), the size and composition of the Federal Reserve's asset holdings, and communications with the public about the likely future course of monetary policy. Congress enacted legislation that created the FOMC as part of the Federal Reserve System in 1933 and 1935.

FOMC Membership

The FOMC consists of 12 voting members—the 7 members of the Board of Governors; the president of the Federal Reserve Bank of New York; and 4 of the remaining 11 Reserve Bank presidents, who serve one-year terms on a rotating basis.

Figure 2.4. Composition of the Federal Open Market Committee

The Federal Open Market Committee's (FOMC) structure promotes the consideration of broad U.S. economic perspectives and the public interest in key monetary policy decisions made by the U.S. central bank.

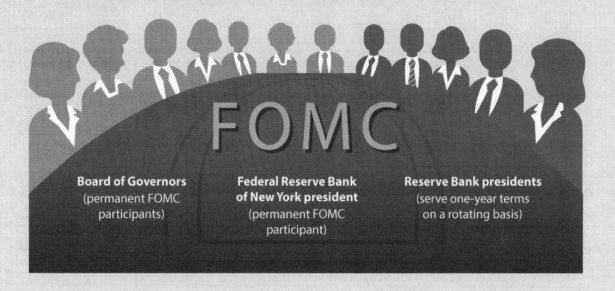

Board of Governors
(permanent FOMC participants)

Federal Reserve Bank of New York president
(permanent FOMC participant)

Reserve Bank presidents
(serve one-year terms on a rotating basis)

All 12 of the Reserve Bank presidents attend FOMC meetings and participate in FOMC discussions, but only the presidents who are Committee members at the time may vote on policy decisions.

By law, the FOMC determines its own internal organization and, by tradition, the FOMC elects the Chair of the Board of Governors as its chair and the president of the Federal Reserve Bank of New York as its vice chair. FOMC meetings are typically held eight times each year in Washington, D.C., and at other times as needed.

FOMC Responsibilities

The FOMC is charged with overseeing "open market operations," the principal tool by which the Federal Reserve executes U.S. monetary policy. These operations affect the federal funds rate, which in turn influence overall monetary and credit conditions, aggregate demand, and

Want to learn more about the FOMC?

For more information about the FOMC, visit the About the Fed section of the Board's website, www.federalreserve.gov/aboutthefed/structure-federal-open-market-committee.htm.

the entire economy (see section 3, "Conducting Monetary Policy," on page 20). The FOMC also directs operations undertaken by the Federal Reserve in foreign exchange markets and, in recent years, has authorized currency swap programs with foreign central banks.

. . . .

Other Significant Entities Contributing to Federal Reserve Functions

Two other groups play important roles in the Federal Reserve System's core functions: (1) depository institutions—banks, thrifts, and credit unions; and (2) Federal Reserve System advisory committees, which make recommendations to the Board of Governors and to the Reserve Banks regarding the System's responsibilities.

Depository Institutions

Depository institutions offer transaction, or checking, accounts to the public and may maintain accounts of their own at their local Federal Reserve Banks. Depository institutions are required to meet reserve requirements—that is, to keep a certain amount of cash on hand or in an account at a Reserve Bank based on the total balances in the checking accounts they hold.

Depository institutions that have higher balances in their Reserve Bank accounts than they need to meet reserve requirements may lend to other depository institutions that need those funds to satisfy their own reserve requirements. This rate influences interest rates, asset prices and wealth, exchange rates, and, thereby, aggregate demand in the economy. The FOMC sets a target for the federal funds rate at its meetings and authorizes actions called open market operations to achieve that target (see section 3, "Conducting Monetary Policy," on page 20 for more information about the conduct of monetary policy).

Advisory Councils

Four advisory committees assist and advise the Board on matters of public policy.

1. **Federal Advisory Council (FAC).** This council, established by the Federal Reserve Act, comprises 12 representatives of the banking industry. The FAC ordinarily meets with the Board four times a year, as required by law. Annually, each Reserve Bank chooses one person to represent its District on the FAC. FAC members customarily serve three one-year terms and elect their own officers.

2. **Community Depository Institutions Advisory Council (CDIAC).** The CDIAC was originally established by the Board of Governors to obtain information and views from thrift institutions (savings and loan institutions and mutual savings banks) and credit unions. More recently, its membership has expanded to include community banks. Like the FAC, the CDIAC provides the Board of Governors with firsthand insight and information about the economy, lending conditions, and other issues.

3. **Model Validation Council.** This council was established by the Board of Governors in 2012 to provide expert and independent advice on its process to rigorously assess the models used in stress tests of banking institutions. Stress tests are required under the Dodd-Frank Wall Street Reform and Consumer Protection Act. The council is intended to improve the quality of stress tests and thereby strengthen confidence in the stress-testing program. (For more information about stress tests, see "Capital Planning, Stress Testing, and Capital Distributions" on page 112.)

4. **Community Advisory Council (CAC).** This council was formed by the Federal Reserve Board in 2015 to offer diverse perspectives on the economic circumstances and financial services needs of consumers and communities, with a particular focus on the concerns of low- and moderate-income populations. The CAC complements the FAC and CDIAC, whose members represent depository institutions.

More on Federal Reserve Advisory Councils

For a current roster of Federal Reserve advisory council members, visit the About the Fed section of the Federal Reserve Board public website at www.federalreserve.gov/aboutthefed/advisorydefault.htm.

The CAC meets semiannually with members of the Board of Governors. The 15 CAC members serve staggered three-year terms and are selected by the Board through a public nomination process.

Federal Reserve Banks also have their own advisory committees. Perhaps the most important of these are committees that advise the Banks on agricultural, small business, and labor matters. The Federal Reserve Board solicits the views of each of these committees biannually.

Function

Conducting Monetary Policy

The Federal Open Market Committee sets U.S. monetary policy in accordance with its mandate from Congress: to promote maximum employment, stable prices, and moderate long-term interest rates in the U.S. economy.

3

*W*hat is monetary policy? It is the Federal Reserve's actions, as a central bank, to achieve three goals specified by Congress: maximum employment, stable prices, and moderate long-term interest rates in the United States (figure 3.1).

The Federal Reserve conducts the nation's monetary policy by managing the level of short-term interest rates and influencing the availability and cost of credit in the economy. Monetary policy directly affects interest rates; it indirectly affects stock prices, wealth, and currency exchange rates. Through these channels, monetary policy influences spending, investment, production, employment, and inflation in the United States. Effective monetary policy complements fiscal policy to support economic growth.

While the Federal Reserve's monetary policy goals have not changed for many years, its tools and approach to implementing policy have evolved

Figure 3.1. The Federal Reserve's statutory mandate

The Federal Reserve conducts monetary policy in pursuit of three goals set for it by Congress. The three mandated goals are considered essential to a well-functioning economy for consumers and businesses.

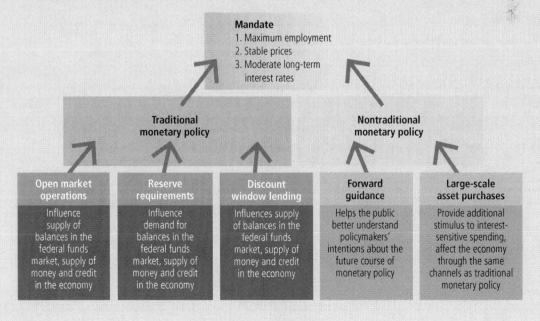

Mandate
1. Maximum employment
2. Stable prices
3. Moderate long-term interest rates

Traditional monetary policy

Nontraditional monetary policy

Open market operations	Reserve requirements	Discount window lending	Forward guidance	Large-scale asset purchases
Influence supply of balances in the federal funds market, supply of money and credit in the economy	Influence demand for balances in the federal funds market, supply of money and credit in the economy	Influences supply of balances in the federal funds market, supply of money and credit in the economy	Helps the public better understand policymakers' intentions about the future course of monetary policy	Provide additional stimulus to interest-sensitive spending, affect the economy through the same channels as traditional monetary policy

over time. Prior to the financial crisis that began in 2007, the Federal Reserve bought or sold securities issued or backed by the U.S. government in the open market on most business days in order to keep a key short-term money market interest rate, called the federal funds rate, at or near a target set by the Federal Open Market Committee, or FOMC (figure 3.2). (The FOMC is the monetary policymaking arm of the Federal Reserve.) Changes in that target, and in investors' expectations of what that target would be in the future, generated changes in a wide range of interest rates paid by borrowers and earned by savers.

To support the economy during the financial crisis that began in 2007 and during the ensuing recession, the FOMC lowered its target for the federal funds rate to near zero at the end of 2008. It then began to use less traditional approaches to implementing policy, including buying very large amounts of longer-term government securities to apply downward pressure on longer-term interest rates. In addition, the Federal Reserve's communication of its assessment of the outlook for the economy and its intentions regarding the federal funds rate became a more important policy tool. In the fall of 2014, with the economy having made substantial progress toward maximum employment, the FOMC announced key elements of its plans for normalizing monetary policy when appropriate. In December 2015, the FOMC decided that economic conditions and the economic outlook warranted starting the process of policy normalization and voted to raise its target for the federal funds rate.

The Federal Reserve's Monetary Policy Mandate and Why It Matters

The Federal Reserve was created by Congress in 1913 to provide the nation with a safer, more flexible, and more stable monetary and financial system. The Federal Reserve Act states that the Board of Governors and the FOMC should conduct monetary policy "so as to promote effectively the goals of maximum employment, stable prices, and moderate long-term interest rates." This statutory mandate ties monetary policy to the broader goal of fostering a productive and stable U.S. economy.

The statutory mandate is achieved when most people looking for work are gainfully employed, and when prices for goods and services are, on average, relatively stable. Stable prices for goods

Figure 3.2. The federal funds rate over time

The effective federal funds rate is the interest rate at which depository institutions—banks, savings institutions (thrifts), and credit unions—and government-sponsored enterprises borrow from and lend to each other overnight to meet short-term business needs. The target for the federal funds rate—which is set by the Federal Open Market Committee—has varied widely over the years in response to prevailing economic conditions.

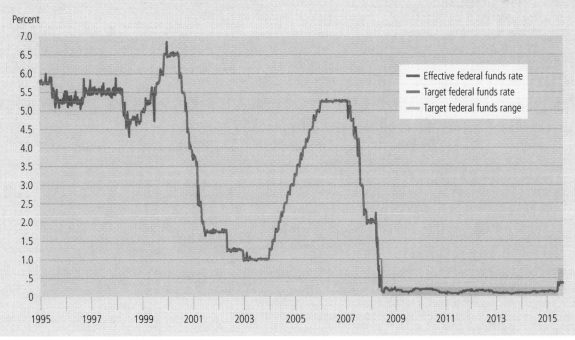

Percent

and services contribute importantly to achieving three economic outcomes: (1) maximum sustainable economic growth, (2) maximum sustainable employment, and (3) moderate long-term interest rates.

When the average of prices of a broad collection of goods and services is stable and believed likely to remain so, changes in the prices of individual goods and services serve as clear guides for efficient resource allocation in the U.S. economy. This then contributes to higher standards of living for U.S. citizens.

Moreover, stable prices encourage saving and capital formation because when the risks of erosion of asset values resulting from inflation—and the need to guard against such losses—are minimized, households are encouraged to save more and businesses are encouraged to invest more.

The Federal Reserve's other responsibilities—promoting financial system stability (section 4), supervising and regulating financial institutions and activities (section 5), fostering payment and settlement system safety and efficiency (section 6), and promoting consumer protection and community development (section 7)—contribute to the nation's economic well-being by supporting a smoothly functioning financial system.

To promote public understanding of how the Federal Reserve interprets its statutory mandate, the FOMC released its "Statement on Longer-Run Goals and Monetary Policy Strategy" in January 2012. This statement explains the FOMC's longer-run goals and its strategy for setting monetary policy to achieve them. In the statement, the FOMC also established a numerical longer-run goal for inflation: In the Committee's judgment, an annual rate of increase of 2 percent in the price index for personal consumption expenditures—an important price measure for consumer spending on goods and services—is most consistent, over the longer run, with meeting the Federal Reserve's statutory mandate to promote both maximum employment and price stability. The FOMC reaffirms its goals statement at its January meeting each year.

Low and stable inflation. Because the nation's inflation rate over the longer run is primarily determined by monetary policy, the Federal Reserve can work directly to ensure that the U.S. economy benefits from low and stable inflation. Low and stable inflation helps the economy operate efficiently. When inflation is low and stable, individuals can hold money without having to worry that high inflation will rapidly erode its purchasing power. Moreover, households and businesses can make more accurate longer-run financial decisions about borrowing and lending and about saving and investment. Longer-term interest rates are also more likely to be moderate when inflation is low and stable.

In contrast, deflation—which occurs when the prices of goods and services are falling, on average—would increase the burden of household and business debts after adjusting for the decline in prices. Moreover, if inflation persisted near zero, short-term interest rates would likely also be quite low and monetary policymakers might not be able to reduce interest rates enough to support the economy when it is at risk of sliding into recession. (Note that the terms "policymakers," "monetary policymakers," and "FOMC policymakers" are used interchangeably in this section.) As a result, monetary policy that aims to keep inflation at 2 percent over the longer run helps to maintain a productive and well-functioning economy, leading to increases in employment and to higher standards of living for U.S. citizens. In this way, the goal of achieving maximum employment in the economy is closely linked with the goal of 2 percent inflation.

Maximum employment. The goal of maximum employment stands on an equal footing with price stability as an objective of monetary policy. However, policymakers recognize that factors other than monetary policy largely determine the maximum level of employment that can be sustained without leading to higher inflation. These factors include trends in the size and makeup of the population, changes in the types of jobs and skills needed in the workforce, and other policies such as those affecting education and training. Consequently, it would not be appropriate for the FOMC to specify a fixed goal for employment.

Policymakers consider a range of indicators in making their assessments of labor market conditions consistent with maximum employment, recognizing that those assessments are necessarily uncertain and may change. All FOMC participants present their views on the longer-run outlook for economic activity and unemployment four times each year, in their Summary of Economic Projections. In those projections, participants report the unemployment rate they expect over the longer run. For example, in the projections released in March 2016, FOMC participants' estimates of the longer-run normal unemployment rate ranged from 4.7 to 5.8 percent, with a median estimate of 4.8 percent.

The Federal Reserve's goals for maximum employment and 2 percent inflation are generally complementary. For example, when inflation is below 2 percent and the FOMC judges that conditions in the labor market are not as strong as those that the Committee views as consistent with maximum employment, the FOMC can keep interest rates temporarily low to promote higher employment and return inflation to 2 percent. Of course, the FOMC may, at times, face situations in which its goals are not complementary; for example, inflation might be above 2 percent even as employment is below its maximum level. The FOMC has indicated in its "Statement on Longer-Run Goals and Monetary Policy Strategy" that, in such a situation, it would follow a balanced approach to achieving its goals, taking into account how close or far employment is from its maximum level and how close or far inflation is from 2 percent. (The "Statement on Longer-Run Goals and Monetary Policy Strategy" is available on the Federal Reserve Board's website at www.federalreserve.gov/monetarypolicy.)

Because monetary policy actions influence inflation and employment with a lag, the FOMC's decisions are based on its assessments of the medium-term outlook for the economy and the potentially different time horizons over which employment and inflation could be expected to return to levels consistent with the Committee's mandate. In addition, the FOMC considers any risks associated with the economic outlook, including risks to the financial system that could impede attaining the Committee's goals.

Longer-run views aid monetary policy

FOMC participants present their views on the longer-run outlook for economic activity and unemployment four times each year in their Summary of Economic Projections, available on the Federal Reserve Board's website at www.federalreserve.gov/ monetarypolicy/ fomccalendars.htm.

Conducting Monetary Policy

How Monetary Policy Affects the Economy

FOMC policymakers set monetary policy to foster financial conditions they judge to be consistent with achieving the Federal Reserve's statutory mandate of maximum employment, stable prices, and moderate long-term interest rates. Monetary policy affects the U.S. economy—and the achievement of the statutory mandate—primarily through its influence on the availability and cost of money and credit in the economy.

As conditions in the economy change, the Committee adjusts monetary policy accordingly, typically by raising or lowering its target for the federal funds rate. A change in the target for the federal funds rate normally will be accompanied by changes in other interest rates and in financial conditions more broadly; those changes will then affect the spending decisions of households and businesses and thus will have implications for economic growth, employment, and inflation.

Effect of Changes in Federal Funds Rate Target on Financial Markets and Spending

Short-term interest rates. Short-term interest rates—for example, the rate of return paid to holders of U.S. Treasury bills or commercial paper (a short-term debt security) issued by private companies—are affected by changes in the level of the federal funds rate.

Short-term interest rates would likely decline if the FOMC reduced its target for the federal funds rate, or if unfolding events or Federal Reserve communications led the public to think that the FOMC would soon reduce the federal funds rate to a level lower than previously expected. Conversely, short-term interest rates would likely rise if the FOMC increased the funds rate target, or if unfolding events or Federal Reserve communications prompted the public to believe that the funds rate would soon be moved to a higher level than had been anticipated.

These changes in short-term market interest rates resulting from a change in the FOMC's target for the federal funds rate typically are transmitted to medium- and longer-term interest rates, such as those on Treasury notes and bonds, corporate bonds, fixed-rate mortgages, and auto and other consumer loans. Medium- and longer-term interest rates are also affected by how people expect the federal funds rate to change in the future. For example, if borrowers and lenders think, today, that the FOMC is likely to raise its target for the federal funds rate substantially over the next several years, then medium-term interest rates today will be appreciably higher than short-term interest rates.

Generally speaking, the effect on short-term interest rates of a single change in the FOMC's target for the federal funds rate will be somewhat larger than the effect on longer-term rates because long-term rates typically reflect the expected course of short-term rates over a long period. However, the influence of a change in the FOMC's target for the federal funds rate on longer-term interest rates can also be substantial if it has clear implications for the expected course of short-term rates over a considerable period.

Longer-term interest rates and stock prices. Changes in longer-term interest rates usually also affect stock prices, and because many individuals hold some stocks either directly or indirectly (through a mutual fund or as part of a pension plan), the change in stock prices will have implications for personal wealth. For example, if longer-term interest rates decline, then investors may decide to purchase stocks, thus bidding up stock prices. Moreover, lower interest rates may lead investors to anticipate that the economy will be stronger and profits will be higher in the future, and this expectation may add further to the demand for stocks.

Dollar exchange rates and international trade. Changes in monetary policy can also affect the value of the U.S. dollar in international currency markets. For example, if monetary policy causes interest rates to fall in the United States, yields on U.S. dollar assets will look less favorable to international investors. With U.S. dollar assets less attrac-

Open market purchases of longer-term securities

Prior to the 2007–09 financial crisis, the Federal Reserve's Open Market Desk typically bought Treasury securities with an average maturity of about three years. Since 2008, the Desk purchased securities with longer remaining maturities in order to increase the effects of the purchases on longer-term interest rates, and purchased mortgage-backed securities to reduce the cost and increase the availability of credit for the purchase of homes.

tive, international investors may invest less in dollar-denominated assets, lowering the value of the dollar in foreign exchange markets. A fall in the value of the dollar will tend to boost U.S. exports because it reduces the price that residents of other countries would need to pay in their own currencies for U.S. goods and services. Moreover, a dollar depreciation means that U.S. residents' purchases of imported products become more expensive, giving U.S. consumers and firms an incentive to purchase domestically produced goods and services instead of foreign ones.

Effects on wealth and spending. Regardless of whether they result from an actual or expected change in monetary policy, the changes in longer-term interest rates, stock prices, and the foreign exchange value of the dollar will affect a wide range of spending decisions made by households and businesses. For example, when the FOMC eases monetary policy (that is, reduces its target for the federal funds rate), lower interest rates on consumer loans will elicit greater spending on durable goods (long-lasting manufactured goods) such as televisions and automobiles. Lower mortgage rates will make buying a house more affordable and lead to more home purchases. In addition, lower mortgage rates will encourage homeowners to refinance their mortgages, freeing up some cash for other purchases. For individuals holding stocks either directly, through mutual funds, or as part of a retirement plan, higher stock prices will add to wealth, helping to spur more spending. Investment projects that businesses previously believed would be only marginally unprofitable will become attractive because of reduced financing costs, particularly if businesses expect their sales to rise.

Degree of Slack or Overheating

FOMC policymakers, in determining the appropriate position or "stance" of monetary policy, must assess the current and likely future degree of slack or overheating in the economy. Because measuring the maximum sustainable level of employment or the potential output of the national economy is a complex undertaking, and inherent uncertainties surround any particular estimate, policymakers consider a wide range of indicators of resource utilization when thinking about appropriate monetary policy.

If resources are underused—for example, employment is below what policymakers judge to be its maximum sustainable level and seems likely to remain below—then they have scope for easing monetary policy to move the economy to its full employment level. Conversely, if resource utilization appears likely to remain above the level associated with maximum employment, then policymakers may judge that a tighter monetary policy is necessary to prevent inflation from rising above 2 percent.

Other Factors Affecting Monetary Policy

Monetary policy affects the economy with a lag. Although the channels through which the FOMC's monetary policy decisions are transmitted to financial conditions and the economy are reasonably straightforward, monetary policy affects the economy with a lag. This means that an FOMC policy decision will not change consumer or business spending immediately. When the FOMC adjusts monetary policy, it expects that the adjustment will affect economic conditions *in the future,* and that those economic conditions will differ from what they would have been in the absence of the policy adjustment. Thus, in setting monetary policy, policymakers must not only evaluate current economic conditions, they must also forecast how the economy is likely to evolve over the next few years.

Anticipated factors. Monetary policy is not the only influence on the economy. Many other factors can affect spending, output, employment, and inflation.

Some of these factors can be anticipated and factored into the FOMC's policymaking. For example, the government influences demand in the economy through changes in taxes and spending programs, which are often anticipated. Indeed, the economic effects of a tax cut may precede its actual implementation if businesses and households increase their spending in anticipation of lower taxes. In addition, forward-looking financial markets may build anticipated fiscal events into the level and structure of interest rates.

Demand shocks. Other factors that affect spending on goods and services can come as a surprise and can influence the economy in unforeseen ways. Examples of these "demand shocks" include shifts in consumer and business confidence or unexpected changes in the credit standards that banks and other lenders apply when they consider making loans. Once a demand shock is identified, monetary policy can be used to address it.

For instance, if consumer and business confidence falter and spending slows, the FOMC can ease monetary policy, lowering interest rates to help move spending back up. But because data and other information on the state of the economy are not available immediately, it can take time before a demand shock is identified and, given that policy actions operate with a lag, an even longer time before it is countered. Thus, demand shocks—even ones that can be addressed by monetary policy—can push the economy away from the Federal Reserve's goals of maximum employment and price stability for a time.

Supply shocks. Other shocks can affect the production of goods and services and their prices by affecting the costs associated with production or the technology used in production.

Examples of such "supply shocks" include crop losses due to extreme weather and slowdowns in productivity growth relative to what would have occurred otherwise—these sorts of adverse supply shocks tend to raise prices and reduce output (and also employment). A disruption in the oil market that reduces the supply of oil and increases its price substantially can also raise other prices and reduce output because oil is an input to the production of many products. In the face of these adverse supply shocks, FOMC policymakers can attempt to counter the loss of output by easing monetary policy and making financial conditions more conducive to spending; alternatively, policymakers can attempt to counter the rise in prices by tightening policy.

As discussed, the FOMC has indicated in its "Statement on Longer-Run Goals and Monetary Policy Strategy" that, in such a situation, it would follow a balanced approach to achieving its goals, taking into account how close or far employment is from its maximum level and how close or far inflation is from 2 percent. Of course, the economy can also experience beneficial supply shocks, such as technological breakthroughs or reductions in the cost of important raw materials, and these beneficial supply shocks can both lower prices and boost output.

Monetary Policy in Practice

How are monetary policy decisions made? The members of the Board of Governors and the presidents of the 12 Federal Reserve Banks gather at the Board's office in Washington, D.C., for eight regularly scheduled meetings of the FOMC each year to discuss economic and financial conditions and deliberate on monetary policy. If necessary, FOMC participants may also meet by video conference at other times. The Federal Reserve Bank of New York carries out the policy decisions made at FOMC meetings primarily by buying and selling securities as authorized by the FOMC.

Overview of the Federal Reserve System and the FOMC

See section 1 for an overview of the Federal Reserve System and the FOMC.

Federal Open Market Committee Meetings

At its meetings, the FOMC considers three key questions: How is the U.S. economy likely to evolve in the near and medium term, what is the appropriate monetary policy setting to help move the economy over the medium term to the FOMC's goals of 2 percent inflation and maximum employment, and how can the FOMC effectively communicate its expectations for the economy and its policy decisions to the public? For a closer look at FOMC meeting deliberations and open market operations, see box 3.1 and figure 3.3, respectively.

Keeping Policy in Step with Evolving Economic Conditions

As discussed, the FOMC's overall approach to its decisionmaking is described in its statement on its longer-run goals and its strategy for

Box 3.1. What Happens at an FOMC Meeting

In preparation for each FOMC meeting, policymakers analyze economic and financial developments and update their forecasts of economic activity, employment, and inflation over the near and medium term. The materials that they and their staffs review include a wide range of U.S. and international economic and financial data, statistical and judgmental economic forecasts, and analyses of alternative policy approaches. Participants also consult business, consumer, and financial industry contacts to hear their perspectives on economic and financial conditions and the outlook.

The staff of the Federal Reserve Banks collect and summarize information on current economic conditions in their Districts. An overall summary, commonly known as the Beige Book, is released to the public one week before the FOMC meeting. (The Beige Book is available at www.federalreserve.gov/monetarypolicy/beigebook/default.htm.) At about the same time, the staff of the Federal Reserve Board distributes to all FOMC participants its analysis of the economy, its economic forecasts, and an analysis of several policy options that span the range of plausible monetary policy responses to the current and expected economic situation. Economic research groups at the Reserve Banks separately brief their Bank presidents on relevant economic developments and policy choices. Using these materials, FOMC participants formulate their preliminary views on the economic outlook and the appropriate policy response in preparation for their meeting in Washington.

During the first part of the meeting, the Federal Reserve governors and Reserve Bank presidents receive briefings that review the operations of the System Open Market Desk at the Federal Reserve Bank of New York and recent economic and financial developments in the United States and abroad. Each Bank president around the table then takes a turn presenting his or her views on economic conditions in his or her District, and both the presidents and governors offer their assessments of recent developments and the outlook.

After a staff presentation on options for monetary policy, participants again share their individual judgments of how policy should be conducted over the period prior to the next FOMC meeting, how they expect policy to evolve over the medium run, and how the Committee's policy intentions should be communicated to the public. While all participants are included in the discussions, the policy decision rests with the voting members of the FOMC—the members of the Board of Governors, the president of the Federal Reserve Bank of New York, and four of the Bank presidents (on a rotating basis).

For more information on the FOMC and other key Federal Reserve entities, see section 2. For an in-depth look at what happens at an FOMC meeting, see the speech that former Federal Reserve Governor Elizabeth A. Duke delivered in October 2010, "Come with Me to the FOMC," available at www.federalreserve.gov/newsevents/speech/duke20101019a.htm.

setting monetary policy to achieve them. In practice, however, selecting policy tools to implement the FOMC's policy strategy is not clear cut. The U.S. and global economies are complex and evolving, and changes in monetary policy take time to affect economic activity, employment, and inflation.

Moreover, monetary policy is just one of the factors determining the pace of domestic economic activity, employment, and inflation. Accordingly, in making their assessment of how the economy is likely to evolve in the near and medium term, policymakers take into account a range of other influences on the economy. Some can readily be built into economic forecasts. For example, federal, state, and local tax and spending policies have important and relatively predictable effects on household and business spending and are typically budgeted in advance. Even so, the range of uncertainty about the effects of some predictable factors may be wide.

And, of course, some economic developments—such as shifts in consumer and business confidence, changes in the terms under which banks extend loans, or disruptions to oil or agricultural supplies—can occur suddenly and with little warning. Finally, the actions of other central banks and fiscal authorities abroad also play a role through the effects on international trade and global financial flows and exchange rates.

How the FOMC Determines Its Monetary Policy Stance

FOMC policymakers use a broad range of information to assess trends in the U.S. economy and to judge the appropriate stance of monetary policy. They analyze the most up-to-date economic data and review reports and surveys from business and financial market contacts. In addition, they use various tools for forecasting economic developments and evaluating the effects of monetary policy decisions. Statistical models can help analyze how changes in economic conditions may affect the outlook for economic activity, employment, and inflation, and how the level of the target federal funds rate might respond to those changes. Simulations of these models, including results using a variety of policy rules that relate the setting of the target federal funds rate to the objectives of monetary policy, can provide some indication of how monetary policy is likely to affect the economy over the longer run.

Because policy actions take time to affect the economy and inflation, policymakers may assess the effects of their policies by looking at various indicators that are likely to respond more quickly to changes in the federal funds rate. Over the years, policymakers have at times monitored indicators such as the monetary aggregates (measures of the

Using statistical models in monetary policy analysis

Federal Reserve staff use statistical economic models to help the FOMC forecast economic developments and evaluate the effects of monetary policy decisions. For more detail on these models, see "The FRB/US Model: A Tool for Macroeconomic Policy Analysis" at www.federalreserve.gov/econresdata/notes/feds-notes/2014/a-tool-for-macroeconomic-policy-analysis.html.

Figure 3.3. How the Federal Reserve conducts open market operations

When the Federal Open Market Committee (FOMC) sets monetary policy that, for example, requires adding liquidity to the banking system to spur economic activity, it instructs the Federal Reserve Bank of New York's (FRBNY) Open Market Desk to purchase U.S. Treasury securities in the open market.

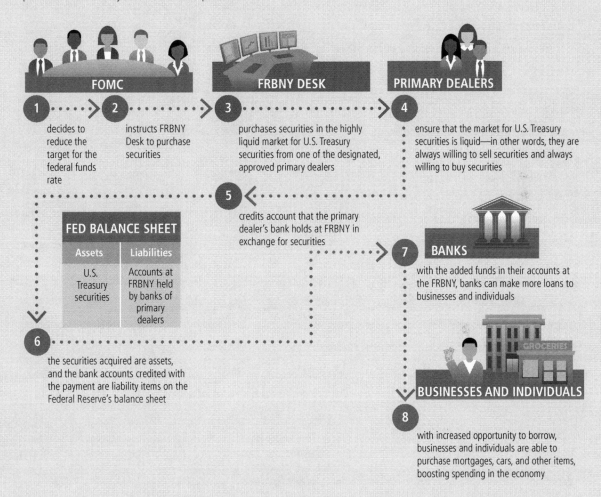

FOMC

1 decides to reduce the target for the federal funds rate

2 instructs FRBNY Desk to purchase securities

FRBNY DESK

3 purchases securities in the highly liquid market for U.S. Treasury securities from one of the designated, approved primary dealers

PRIMARY DEALERS

4 ensure that the market for U.S. Treasury securities is liquid—in other words, they are always willing to sell securities and always willing to buy securities

5 credits account that the primary dealer's bank holds at FRBNY in exchange for securities

FED BALANCE SHEET

Assets	Liabilities
U.S. Treasury securities	Accounts at FRBNY held by banks of primary dealers

6 the securities acquired are assets, and the bank accounts credited with the payment are liability items on the Federal Reserve's balance sheet

BANKS

7 with the added funds in their accounts at the FRBNY, banks can make more loans to businesses and individuals

BUSINESSES AND INDIVIDUALS

8 with increased opportunity to borrow, businesses and individuals are able to purchase mortgages, cars, and other items, boosting spending in the economy

Note: A more detailed explanation of open market operations, including information on the Open Market Desk's purchases and sales of securities, is available on the website of the Federal Reserve Bank of New York, www.newyorkfed.org/markets/.

stock of money), changes in Treasury yields and private-sector interest rates and the levels of those rates for securities that mature at different times in the future, and exchange rates. Importantly, to be valuable to policymakers, these and other possible policy guides must have a close, predictable relationship with the ultimate goals of monetary policy, but this has not always been the case.

Forward Guidance Signals
the FOMC's Policy Intentions

In addition to adjusting the target for the federal funds rate, the FOMC also can influence financial conditions by communicating how it intends to adjust policy in the future. Since March 2009, when the federal funds rate was effectively at its lower bound, this form of communication, called "forward guidance," has been an important signal to the public of the FOMC's policy intentions. For example, when the FOMC said in its March 2009 postmeeting statement that it intended to keep the target for the federal funds rate "exceptionally low" for "an extended period," its goal was to cause financial market participants to adjust their expectations to assume a longer period of lower short-term interest rates than they had previously expected and, thus, put downward pressure on long-term interest rates to provide more support for the economic recovery.

Between 2009 and 2014, the FOMC revised its forward guidance several times, strengthening its intent to put downward pressure on interest rates when the economy appeared to be operating at a lower level than desirable and, more recently, revising it to clarify how, when the time was appropriate, the Committee would make the decision to raise the target federal funds rate.

What Monetary Policymakers
Say to the Public

While the use of forward guidance as a policy tool is relatively new, the Federal Reserve has had a long-standing commitment to communicate regularly with the public and Congress concerning its monetary policy activities and the pursuit of its mandate. While some communications are required by statute, most represent an effort by the Federal Reserve to increase the transparency of its policy decisions and operations.

Statements after FOMC meetings. Since 1994, the Federal Reserve has issued statements announcing FOMC decisions. In recent years, those statements have summarized the Committee's judgment about the appropriate conduct of monetary policy over the intermeeting

FOMC postmeeting statements

The release of postmeeting communications often provides the broader context for FOMC policy decisions. See the FOMC's most recent postmeeting statement at www.federalreserve.gov/ monetarypolicy/ fomccalendars.htm. For more detailed information on the history of FOMC communications, see "A Modern History of FOMC Communication: 1975–2002" at www.federalreserve. gov/monetarypolicy/files/ FOMC20030624memo01. pdf.

period and provided guidance about the factors that the FOMC will consider in setting policy as economic and financial developments evolve. The postmeeting statements also indicate which FOMC members voted for an action, and which members, if any, dissented from it. At times, the FOMC also issues broader statements that represent the consensus of almost all participants. An example of a consensus statement is the "Statement on Longer-Run Goals and Monetary Policy Strategy" that was discussed earlier in this section.

Meeting minutes. Detailed minutes of FOMC meetings are released three weeks after each meeting. The minutes cover all policy-related topics that receive a significant amount of attention during the meeting. They describe the views expressed by the participants, the risks and uncertainties attending the outlook, and the reasons for the Committee's decisions. The minutes can help the public interpret economic and financial developments and better understand the Committee's decisions. As an official record of the meeting, the minutes identify all attendees and include votes on all authorized policy operations.

Summary of Economic Projections. Beginning in late 2007, Federal Reserve policymakers began to publish economic projections, the "Summary of Economic Projections," four times each year. Those projections, published along with the FOMC postmeeting statement, now provide participants' assessments of the most likely outcomes for real gross domestic product growth, the unemployment rate, inflation, and the federal funds rate over the medium term and over the longer run. Each participant bases his or her projection on his or her assessment of appropriate monetary policy and assumptions about the factors likely to affect economic outcomes. In April 2011, the Federal Reserve Chair began to hold press briefings following each of the four FOMC meetings per year at which participants provide their projections. At the press conferences, the Chair discusses current and prospective monetary policy and presents a summary of the participants' projections.

Testimonies to Congress, speeches, and transcripts. The FOMC's communication of its policy actions and intentions extends well beyond

---

FOMC postmeeting press conferences

In April 2011, the Federal Reserve Chair began to hold press briefings following each of the four FOMC meetings per year at which participants provide their economic projections. For more information, see www.federalreserve.gov/monetarypolicy/fomccalendars.htm.

the postmeeting statements and minutes. By statute, the Federal
Reserve Chair testifies twice each year on economic developments and
monetary policy before the congressional committees that oversee
the Federal Reserve. At those times, the Board of Governors delivers
the semiannual *Monetary Policy Report* to Congress that discusses the
conduct of monetary policy and economic developments and prospects
for the future. In addition, the Chair and other Board members appear
frequently before Congress to report and answer questions on economic and financial market developments and on monetary and regulatory policy. Many Federal Reserve policymakers regularly give public
speeches. And a wide range of documents, including transcripts of the
FOMC meetings, is made available after a five-year lag.

Communicating with other organizations. Federal Reserve officials
also maintain regular channels of communication with officials of other
U.S. and foreign government agencies, international organizations, and
foreign central banks on subjects of mutual concern.

Although the Federal Reserve's policy objectives are limited to economic
outcomes in the United States, it is mutually beneficial for macroeconomic and financial policymakers in the United States and in other
countries to maintain a continuous dialogue. This dialogue enables
the Federal Reserve to better understand and anticipate influences on
the U.S. economy that emanate from abroad. It also helps the Federal
Reserve and other central banks work together to address common
economic challenges and threats to the global financial system.

· ·

Monetary Policy Implementation

The Federal Funds Market

At the end of any business day, a depository institution may need to
borrow funds overnight to make payments on its own behalf or on
behalf of its customers, to cover a shortfall in its balances held at the

**What is a depository
institution?**

Depository institutions
(also referred to as banks
interchangeably here) include
commercial banks, savings
institutions, credit unions,
and U.S. branches and agencies of foreign banks. In early
2016, there were more than
12,500 depository institutions in the United States
with accounts at the Federal
Reserve.

Box 3.2. Banks Must Meet Reserve Requirements Set by the Federal Reserve Board

The Federal Reserve Board, by law, sets reserve requirements on all depository institutions: They are required to hold cash in their vaults or reserve balances at the Federal Reserve (or a combination of the two) in an amount equal to a certain fraction of their deposits.

Since the early 1990s, these requirements have been applied only to the transaction deposits held at banks—that is, accounts such as checking accounts or interest-bearing accounts that offer unlimited checking privileges. The Board sets a required reserve ratio within limits prescribed by the Federal Reserve Act, and that ratio determines the fraction of deposits that a bank must hold as vault cash or reserve balances. The Federal Reserve infrequently adjusts the required reserve ratio.

A bank may choose to hold reserve balances in excess of the requirement as a means of protecting against an overdraft in its Federal Reserve account or to reduce the risk of failing to hold enough balances to satisfy its reserve requirement. More generally, a bank's desired level of reserve balances is likely to depend upon the volume of, and uncertainty about, payments flowing through its Federal Reserve account.

To read more about reserve requirements, see the Federal Reserve Board's website at www.federalreserve. gov/monetarypolicy/reservereq.htm. Additional discussion about the evolution of reserve requirements can be found in the Federal Reserve Bulletin reports "Open Market Operations in the 1990s," www.federalreserve. gov/pubs/bulletin/1997/199711lead. pdf and "Reserve Requirements: History, Current Practice, and Potential Reform," www.federalreserve.gov/ monetarypolicy/0693lead.pdf.

Federal Reserve, or to meet reserve requirements imposed by the Federal Reserve Board (see box 3.2). An institution that finds itself with excess funds on hand at the end of the business day can arrange to lend those funds overnight to another depository institution in the federal funds market. When banks borrow and lend in the federal funds market, the exchange of funds is reflected in the accounts they hold at the Federal Reserve—funds banks hold in these accounts are known as reserve balances. Since late 2008, the Federal Reserve has paid interest on banks' reserve balances (for a discussion, see box 3.3).

In many ways, this process is analogous to what happens when an individual makes a private loan to another individual. When one person borrows from another, balances from the checking account of the lender are transferred to the checking account of the borrower. Similarly, when a depository institution lends funds to another depository institution in the federal funds market, reserve balances in the lender's "checking account" at the Federal Reserve are transferred to the Federal Reserve account of the borrower.

To be more precise, only depository institutions (banks, savings institutions, credit unions, and U.S. branches of foreign banks) and selected other institutions (the Federal Home Loan Banks and other government-sponsored enterprises) are permitted to hold accounts at the Federal Reserve. Banks use these accounts to make and receive payments in much the same way that a customer would use his or her checking account at a commercial bank. The interest rate on federal funds transactions is called the federal funds rate. For many years before the 2007–09 financial crisis, the FOMC carried out monetary policy by setting a target for the federal funds rate.

Monetary Policy before the 2007–09 Financial Crisis

Open market operations. Over the years, the Federal Reserve has relied upon open market operations to manage conditions in the federal funds market and to keep the federal funds rate at the target level set by the FOMC. The Open Market Desk (the Desk) at the Federal Reserve Bank of New York conducts open market operations by buying or selling securities issued or guaranteed by the U.S. Treasury or U.S. government agencies (figure 3.4).

Box 3.3. The Federal Reserve Pays Interest on Required Reserve Balances and Excess Balances

In 2006, Congress authorized the Federal Reserve to pay interest on reserve balances beginning in 2011. However, the Emergency Economic Stabilization Act of 2008 accelerated this authority, and the Federal Reserve began paying interest on reserve balances in October 2008. The Federal Reserve also pays interest on balances held in excess of the reserve requirement. The interest rates on reserve balances and on excess balances are both set by the Board of Governors.

The payment of interest on balances maintained to satisfy reserve balance requirements is intended to eliminate or reduce the implicit tax that reserve requirements impose on depository institutions. The interest rate paid on excess balances gives the Federal Reserve an additional tool for the conduct of monetary policy. By raising or lowering the interest rate paid on excess reserves (the IOER rate), the Federal Reserve can change the attractiveness of holding excess balances and thus affect the federal funds rate and other short-term market interest rates.

More detailed information on the interest on required reserve balances and excess reserve balances is available on the Federal Reserve Board's website at www.federalreserve.gov/monetary policy/reqresbalances.htm.

The Federal Reserve Act requires that the Desk conduct its purchases and sales in the open market. To do so, the Desk has established relationships with securities dealers known as primary dealers that are active in the market for U.S. government securities. For example, in an open market purchase, the Desk would buy eligible securities from primary dealers (at prices determined in a competitive auction). The Federal Reserve would pay for those securities by crediting the reserve accounts that the banks used by the primary dealers maintain at the Federal Reserve. (The banks, in turn, would credit the dealers' bank accounts.) In this way, the open market purchase leads to an increase in reserve balances. A greater supply of reserve balances would tend to put downward pressure on the federal funds rate, as banks would be willing to lend their excess funds at somewhat lower interest rates. In contrast, an open market sale would reduce reserve balances and put upward pressure on the federal funds rate. Each business day, the

Figure 3.4. Traditional monetary policy: Tools for achieving the targeted federal funds rate

Tool	What is it?	How does it work?	Who uses it?
Reserve requirements	The percentage of deposits that commercial banks and other depository institutions must hold as reserves.	Reserve requirements create a stable demand for reserves. The Federal Reserve then adjusts the supply of reserves through open market operations to keep the level of the federal funds rate close to the target rate established by the Federal Open Market Committee (FOMC).	Determined by the Board of Governors (within ranges specified by the Federal Reserve Act).
Open market operations	Purchases or sales—temporary or permanent—of U.S. government and agency securities in the open market.	Each purchase or sale of securities directly affects the volume of reserves in the banking system and thus the level of the federal funds rate.	Directed by the FOMC; conducted by the Federal Reserve Bank of New York (in competitive operations with primary dealers).
Discount window lending	Depository institutions can borrow from a Federal Reserve Bank.	Credit provided by the Federal Reserve's discount window supplies balances and can help address pressures in the federal funds market.	Reserve Banks lend to depository institutions; interest rate charged is determined by the Board of Governors.

Box 3.4. Discount Window Lending as a Monetary Policy Tool

When the Federal Reserve Act became law in 1913, the Federal Reserve was authorized to lend only to banks that were members of the Federal Reserve System. At the time, this included all nationally chartered banks and those state-chartered banks that had chosen to join the System. Today, by law, all depository institutions that offer transactions accounts subject to reserve requirements can borrow from the Federal Reserve.

At first, the Federal Reserve lent primarily by "discounting" short-term commercial loans owned by banks. In essence, the Federal Reserve made a loan by purchasing the commercial loans for less than their face value, with the difference between the purchase price and the face value (the discount) representing interest the Federal Reserve received on its loan. Originally, these loans were made at a special lending window at each of the Reserve Banks called the discount window. For that reason, over time, Federal Reserve lending to depository institutions became known as "discount window lending." Today, most extensions of credit by the Federal Reserve are made in the form of advances—loans backed by collateral pledged by the borrower—rather than as discounts, but the term "discount window" is still used to refer to the

facilities through which the Federal Reserve lends to depository institutions. Because a bank would be unlikely to borrow in the federal funds market at an interest rate much higher than the discount rate, the availability of discount window loans at an interest rate above the targeted federal funds rate has acted as an upper limit on the funds rate and helped to keep it close to the FOMC's target. The volume of discount window lending and borrowing is usually relatively small.

Depository institutions have access to three types of discount window lending—primary credit, secondary credit, and seasonal credit.

Primary credit is available to generally sound depository institutions on a very short-term basis, typically overnight, but at times for longer periods. To

assess whether a depository institution is in sound financial condition, its Reserve Bank regularly reviews the institution's condition, using supervisory ratings and data on the adequacy of the institution's capital. Depository institutions are not required to seek alternative sources of funds before requesting occasional advances of primary credit, but primary credit is expected to be used as a backup source of funding rather than a routine one. Because primary credit is the Federal Reserve's main discount window program, the Federal Reserve and others in the banking industry at times use the term "discount rate" specifically to refer to the primary credit rate.

Secondary credit may be available to depository institutions that are eligible to borrow from the discount window but that do not meet the criteria for

(continued on the next page)

Desk would determine the quantity of open market operations necessary to keep the federal funds rate at the FOMC's target after taking into account factors in the market for federal funds, including banks' estimated funding needs.

Discount window lending. If a depository institution finds that its need for overnight funding cannot be satisfied in the federal funds market or similar markets, it can borrow from the Federal Reserve's discount window, and the proceeds of the loan would be added to the institution's balance in its reserve account at the Federal Reserve. Rules primary credit. Secondary credit is extended on a very short-term basis, typically overnight. The financial condition of secondary credit borrowers is generally less sound than the financial condition of primary credit borrowers. For that reason, the rate on secondary credit has typically been 50 basis points above the primary credit rate—to compensate for the greater risk of credit loss, although the spread can vary as circumstances warrant. Secondary credit is available to help a depository institution meet backup liquidity needs when its use is consistent with the borrowing institution's timely return to a reliance on market sources of funding or with the orderly resolution of a troubled institution's difficulties. Secondary credit may not be used to fund an expansion of the borrower's assets.

Seasonal credit is designed to help small depository institutions manage significant seasonal swings in their loans and deposits. Seasonal credit is available to depository institutions that can demonstrate a clear pattern of recurring swings in funding needs

throughout the year—these institutions are usually located in agricultural or tourist areas. Borrowing longer-term funds from the discount window during periods of seasonal need allows institutions to carry fewer liquid assets during the rest of the year and makes more funds available for local lending. The seasonal credit rate is based on market interest rates.

Credit terms. By law, depository institutions that have either transaction accounts or nonpersonal time deposits that are subject to reserve requirements may borrow from the discount window. U.S. branches and agencies of foreign banks with transaction accounts or nonpersonal time deposits are also eligible to borrow under the same general terms and conditions that apply to domestic depository institutions.

By law, all discount window loans must be secured to the satisfaction of the lending Reserve Bank. The Federal Reserve generally accepts as collateral for discount window loans any assets that meet regulatory standards

for sound asset quality. This category of assets includes most performing loans and most high-grade securities. Reserve Banks must be able to establish a legal right to be first in line to take possession of and, if necessary, sell all collateral that secures discount window loans in the event of default. The collateral cannot be an obligation of the pledging institution.

Assets accepted as collateral are assigned a lendable value deemed appropriate by the Reserve Bank. Lendable value is the maximum loan amount that can be backed by that asset and is calculated as the value of the asset, less a deducted amount referred to as the "haircut"—that is, the loan is limited relative to the value of the collateral to provide a cushion in case the value of the collateral falls. This haircut helps to protect the Federal Reserve from loss should the borrower fail to repay the loan.

governing access to the discount window are established by the Federal Reserve Act and by the regulations issued by the Board of Governors; after posting collateral, depository institutions can borrow from the discount window at interest rates set by the Reserve Banks, subject to review and determination by the Board.

Since early 2003, interest rates for discount window loans have been set above the target for the federal funds rate. As a result, depository institutions have generally borrowed from the discount window in significant volume only when overall market conditions have tightened enough to push the federal funds rate above the discount rate. Prior to the financial crisis that began in the summer of 2007, discount window borrowing was infrequent (see box 3.4 for additional detail).

Monetary Policy during and after the 2007–09 Financial Crisis

The crisis in global financial markets that began during the summer of 2007 became particularly severe during 2008. One way that the Federal Reserve responded to the crisis was by expanding its lending through the discount window to banks that were experiencing shortages of liquidity. In addition, the Federal Reserve introduced a variety of programs, using legal authority provided by Congress in several sections

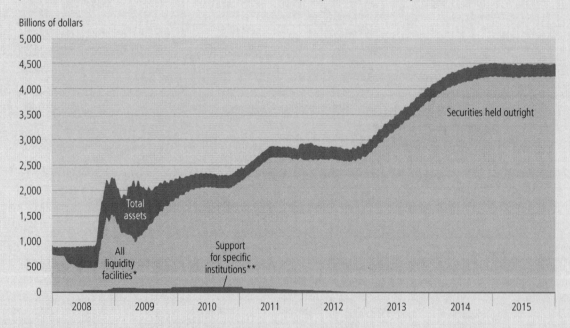

Figure 3.5. Selected assets of the Federal Reserve, August 2007–December 2015

As the 2007–09 crisis intensified, the Federal Reserve introduced a variety of programs—and expanded its balance sheet in the process—to address financial institutions' need for short-term liquidity and strains in many markets.

Billions of dollars

* "All liquidity facilities" includes term auction credit, primary credit, secondary credit, seasonal credit, Primary Dealer Credit Facility, Asset-Backed Commercial Paper Money Market Mutual Fund Liquidity Facility, Term Asset-Backed Securities Loan Facility, Commercial Paper Funding Facility, and central bank liquidity swaps.

** "Support for specific institutions" includes Maiden Lane LLC, Maiden Lane II LLC, Maiden Lane III LLC, and support to American International Group (AIG).

Source: Board of Governors of the Federal Reserve System, statistical release H.4.1, "Factors Affecting Reserve Balances," www.federalreserve.gov/releases/h41.

Conducting Monetary Policy

of the Federal Reserve Act, which were designed to address financial institutions' need for short-term liquidity and strains in many markets.

The Federal Reserve also established dollar liquidity swap arrangements with several foreign central banks to address dollar funding pressures abroad. These programs are discussed in greater detail in box 3.5 "Extraordinary Liquidity Provision during the 2007–09 Financial Crisis." Together, these policy initiatives greatly increased the size of the Federal Reserve's balance sheet as shown in figure 3.5. (For more detail on the balance sheet, see the discussion on page 52 and box 3.6 on page 53 "Understanding the Federal Reserve's Balance Sheet.")

Figure 3.6. Reaching the "zero bound"

The federal funds rate neared its "zero bound" in December 2008. Around that time, the Federal Reserve began to use nontraditional policy tools to boost economic activity.

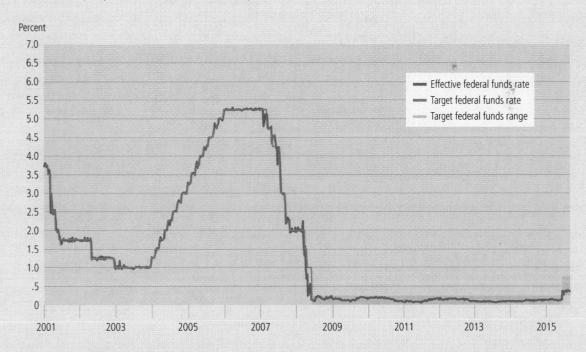

Source: Intended federal funds rate. See the Monetary Policy section of the Board's website, www.federalreserve.gov. For the federal funds rate target, see www.federalreserve.gov/monetarypolicy/openmarket.htm. For the federal funds effective rate, see https://apps.newyorkfed.org/markets/autorates/fed%20funds.

Box 3.5. Extraordinary Liquidity Provision during the 2007–09 Financial Crisis

In response to the financial crisis, the Federal Reserve provided liquidity to firms and markets in a variety of ways. Initially, the Federal Reserve eased the terms on primary credit, the principal type of discount window credit that the Federal Reserve extends to depository institutions. As the crisis intensified, however, the Federal Reserve provided liquidity in nontraditional ways to firms and markets outside of the banking system.

In some cases, the Federal Reserve used its regular authorities in new ways. Even after easing the terms on primary credit, banks were highly reluctant to borrow primary credit out of concern that borrowing from the Federal Reserve would indicate that the bank was experiencing financial difficulties. As a result, the eased terms on primary credit did not significantly reduce the pressures on bank funding markets. To address the banks' concerns, the Federal Reserve conducted regular auctions of fixed quantities of discount window credit. Because the credit was extended through a market mechanism, and because funds were provided several days after the auction, banks were less concerned that borrowing would signal weakness and were less reluctant to borrow. At the same time, because dollar funding markets are global, strains in foreign dollar markets were contributing to volatility in U.S. financial markets. To counter these strains, the Federal Reserve established foreign currency swap lines with several foreign central banks. Under the lines, the Federal Reserve provided the foreign central bank with dollars, which those central banks could lend to financial institutions in their local markets, and received foreign currency in exchange.

During the financial crisis, the Federal Reserve used its emergency lending

(continued on the next page)

Another way that the Federal Reserve responded to the crisis was through its traditional policy tool, the federal funds rate. Beginning in the fall of 2007, the FOMC cut its target for the federal funds rate and by the end of 2008, that target had been reduced from 5¼ percent to a range of 0 to ¼ percentage point (figure 3.6). While this monetary easing was substantial, with the federal funds rate at nearly zero, the FOMC could no longer rely on reducing that rate to provide much further support for the economy.

Although the Federal Reserve's initial responses to the crisis helped financial markets to recover and function more normally, the recession in the U.S. economy that began in December of 2007 was particularly severe and long-lasting. With the federal funds rate near zero, the FOMC turned to two less conventional policy measures—large-scale asset purchases and forward guidance.

Large-scale asset purchases. In late 2008, the Federal Reserve began purchasing longer-term securities through a series of large-scale asset

Conducting Monetary Policy

authority to establish broad-based lending facilities to provide liquidity to financial markets other than the interbank market that were important for the provision of credit to U.S. businesses and households. In particular, many critical financial institutions that depended on short-term funding were not depository institutions and so could not borrow from the discount window when the liquidity of short-term funding markets deteriorated. Moreover, a material fraction of business and household loans were funded through securitizations; when markets for securitized products deteriorated, the supply of credit to businesses and households declined, further weakening the economy. Federal Reserve emergency lending facilities were established to provide liquidity to the market for repurchase agreements, or repos, the commercial paper market, and the asset-backed securities market. A facility was also established to help money market mutual funds meet the heavy withdrawals that occurred after the failure of Lehman Brothers.

Lastly, the Federal Reserve used its emergency authority to provide support to certain specific institutions in order to avert disorderly failures that could have led to even more severe dislocations and strains for the financial system as a whole and harmed the U.S. economy.

All Federal Reserve lending during the financial crisis was well collateralized and every loan was repaid in full, on time, and with interest. In most cases, the interest rate charged on the loans was above those that prevailed in normal times. As a consequence, the lending wound down, with many borrowers even repaying their loans early, as the financial situation improved. Similarly, all dollar liquidity provided to foreign central banks via the swap lines was repaid, and the Federal Reserve earned fees for providing the service. As shown in figure 3.5 on page 44, liquidity provision through broad-based facilities peaked at about $1.5 trillion in early 2009. For detailed information on these liquidity provisions, see the Federal Reserve Board's website at www. federalreserve.gov/monetarypolicy/bst. htm.

purchase programs, thereby putting downward pressure on longer-term interest rates, easing broader financial market conditions, and thus supporting economic activity and job creation. Between December 2008 and August 2010, the Federal Reserve purchased $175 billion in direct obligations of the government-sponsored entities Fannie Mae, Freddie Mac, and the Federal Home Loan Banks as well as $1.25 trillion in mortgage-backed securities (MBS) guaranteed by Fannie Mae, Freddie Mac, and Ginnie Mae. These purchases were intended to help reduce the cost and increase the availability of credit for the purchase of homes.

In addition, between March 2009 and October 2009, the Federal Reserve purchased $300 billion of longer-term Treasury securities. Later, in the face of a sluggish economic recovery, the Federal Reserve expanded its asset holdings in a second purchase program between November 2010 and June 2011, buying an additional $600 billion of longer-term Treasury securities.

Maturity extension program. Between September 2011 and December 2012, the Federal Reserve undertook a "maturity extension program" or MEP. Under the MEP, the Federal Reserve bought $667 billion of Treasury securities with remaining maturities of 6 to 30 years and sold an equivalent value of Treasury securities with remaining maturities of 3 years or less. The MEP added to the downward pressure on longer-term interest rates without affecting the size of the Federal Reserve's balance sheet.

Open-ended asset purchases. Finally, with considerable slack remaining in the economy (as evidenced by an unemployment rate of more than 8 percent), in September 2012 the FOMC began making additional purchases of MBS at a pace of $40 billion per month. In January 2013, these MBS purchases were supplemented by $45 billion per month in purchases of longer-term Treasury securities. Unlike its first two asset purchase programs and the MEP, in which the total size of the program was announced at the time the program was undertaken, the Federal Reserve's third asset purchase program was open-ended. The FOMC indicated that it would continue to purchase assets until the outlook for the labor market had improved substantially so long as inflation and expected inflation remained stable, and so long as the benefits of the purchases continued to outweigh their costs and risks.

In December 2013, the FOMC began to slow the pace of its asset purchases. It continued to slow the pace of purchases at its subsequent meetings, concluding its third asset purchase program in October 2014. Box 3.6 illustrates the effects of the Federal Reserve's asset purchase programs on its holdings of securities (on the asset side of the balance sheet) and the corresponding increase in deposits of depository institutions or reserve balances (on the liability side of the balance sheet).

Since the summer of 2010, the Federal Reserve has continued to reinvest the proceeds of securities that mature or prepay. Maturing Treasury securities are reinvested in Treasury securities, while principal payments on holdings of agency debt and agency MBS are reinvested in agency MBS. By reinvesting, the Federal Reserve continues to hold a large

Reinvestment to slow as the economy improves

The FOMC indicated in December 2015 that it expects to cease or commence phasing out reinvestments well after it begins increasing the target range for the federal funds rate. The timing of this step will depend on how economic and financial conditions and the economic outlook evolve.

amount of longer-term securities and thereby maintains downward pressure on longer-term interest rates.

Forward guidance. In addition to its asset purchase programs, the FOMC used "forward guidance"—that is, it provided information about its intentions for the federal funds rate—to influence expectations about the future course of monetary policy. In December 2008, when the Committee reduced the target for the federal funds rate to nearly zero, it indicated in its postmeeting statement that it expected that "weak economic conditions are likely to warrant exceptionally low levels of the federal funds rate for some time." As the economic effects of the crisis worsened, the FOMC amended its forward guidance in order to help the public understand the Committee's thinking about the future course of policy.

The forward guidance language in the FOMC's postmeeting statement has taken different forms since the onset of the financial crisis. In March 2009, as the economic downturn worsened, the Committee changed the forward guidance to indicate that the federal funds rate could remain at exceptionally low levels "for an extended period." In August 2011, the Committee began using calendar dates in its policy statement in order to indicate the period over which it expected economic conditions to warrant maintaining the federal funds rate near zero. As economic conditions did not improve in line with the Committee's expectations, the calendar date in the forward guidance was extended.

Later, in its December 2012 statement, the FOMC replaced the date-based forward guidance with language indicating the economic conditions that the Committee expected to see before it would begin to consider raising its target for the federal funds rate. When the Committee added the economic conditionality to its statement in December 2012, it also indicated a variety of other economic factors that it would take into account before raising interest rates.

The FOMC's communications about likely future settings of its target for the federal funds rate and its other policy tools have continued to evolve. In particular, since the Committee began to normalize monetary policy by modestly raising its target for the federal funds rate in December of 2015, it has indicated that monetary policy is not on a predetermined path and that its policy decisions will depend on what incoming information tells policymakers about whether a change in policy is necessary to move the economy toward, or keep it at, maximum employment and 2 percent inflation.

Monetary Policy Normalization

Monetary policy has been consistently accommodative in recent years as the FOMC sought to counter the economic effects of the financial crisis and support the recovery from the Great Recession. In late 2015, when the unemployment rate was at or near levels that policymakers judge consistent with maximum employment, the Federal Reserve began taking steps to "normalize" the stance of monetary policy in order to continue to foster its macroeconomic objectives. The term "normalization" refers to steps the FOMC is taking to return short-term interest rates to more-normal levels and reduce the size of the Federal Reserve's balance sheet.

In December 2015, the FOMC began the normalization process by raising its target range for the federal funds rate by ¼ percentage point—the first change since December 2008—bringing the target range to 25 to 50 basis points. The FOMC based its decision on the considerable improvement in labor market conditions during 2015 and reasonable confidence that inflation, which had been running below the Committee's objective, would rise to 2 percent over the medium term. During normalization, the FOMC is continuing to set a target range for the federal funds rate and communicate its policy through this rate. To keep the federal funds rate in its target range, the Federal Reserve uses two administered rates, the interest rate the Federal Reserve pays on excess reserve balances (the IOER rate, discussed in box 3.3 "The Federal Reserve Pays Interest on Required Reserve Balances and Excess

What is a reverse repurchase agreement?

In a reverse repurchase agreement, or "reverse repo," the Federal Reserve Open Market Desk sells a security to an eligible reverse repo counterparty with an agreement to purchase it back at a specified date in the future. For more detailed information on reverse repos or the Federal Reserve's overnight reverse repo facility, see www.federalreserve.gov/ monetarypolicy/overnight-reverse-repurchase-agreements.htm.

Balances" on page 40) and the interest rate it pays on overnight reverse repurchase agreements (the ON RRP rate).

Overnight reverse repurchases. During normalization, the Committee is using an overnight reverse repurchase (ON RRP) facility as a supplementary tool as needed to help control the federal funds rate.

In an ON RRP operation, an eligible financial counterparty provides funds to the Federal Reserve in exchange for Treasury securities on the Federal Reserve's balance sheet and is paid the ON RRP rate; the following day, the funds are returned to the counterparty and the securities are returned to the Federal Reserve. In general, any counterparty that is eligible to participate in ON RRP operations should be unwilling to invest funds overnight with another counterparty at a rate below the ON RRP rate. The FOMC plans to use the ON RRP facility only to the extent necessary and will phase it out when it is no longer needed to help control the funds rate.

Policy implementation during normalization. By paying interest on reserves and offering ON RRPs, the Federal Reserve is providing safe, liquid investments for banking institutions and ON RRP counterparties. The Federal Reserve intends to set the IOER rate equal to the top of the FOMC's target range for the federal funds rate and the ON RRP rate equal to the bottom of the target range. Increasing these two rates puts upward pressure on short-term market rates, including the federal funds rate, as investors are less willing to accept a lower rate elsewhere.

Other policy tools. Other supplementary tools, such as term deposits offered through the Federal Reserve's Term Deposit Facility and term reverse repurchase agreements, will also be used, if needed, to put upward pressure on money market interest rates and so help to control the federal funds rate and keep it in the target range set by the FOMC. Term deposits are like interest-bearing certificates of deposit that depository institutions hold at Federal Reserve Banks for a specified length of time; the Board of Governors sets the interest rate on term deposits. Funds placed in term deposits are transferred from the reserve

The Federal Reserve's changing approach to policy implementation

For a primer on the framework the Federal Reserve is using for monetary policy normalization, see "Monetary Policy 101: The Fed's Changing Approach to Policy Implementation" at www.federalreserve.gov/econresdata/feds/2015/files/2015047pap.pdf.

balances of participating institutions into a term deposit account at the Federal Reserve for the life of the term deposit, thereby draining reserves from the banking system.

The balance sheet. As the policy normalization process proceeds, the Federal Reserve's securities holdings—and the supply of reserve balances—will be reduced in a gradual and predictable manner primarily by ceasing to reinvest repayments of principal on securities held in the portfolio. As of October 2016, the FOMC had not decided when to begin tapering or ceasing its reinvestments and did not anticipate selling agency MBS as part of the normalization process, although limited sales might be warranted in the longer run to reduce or eliminate residual holdings. The FOMC will announce the timing and pace of any sales in advance.

The FOMC intends that the Federal Reserve will, over the longer run, hold no more securities than necessary to implement monetary policy efficiently and effectively, and that it will hold primarily Treasury securities, thereby minimizing the effect of Federal Reserve holdings on the allocation of credit across sectors of the economy.

Box 3.6. Understanding the Federal Reserve's Balance Sheet

The Federal Reserve's balance sheet, published weekly, contains a great deal of information about the scale and scope of its operations. For decades, market participants have closely studied the evolution of the Federal Reserve's balance sheet to understand important details about the implementation of monetary policy.

The table below shows the major asset and liability categories on the Federal Reserve's balance sheet. Conventional open market operations and large-scale asset purchases affect the Federal Reserve's balance sheet in a similar fashion. For example, when the Open Market Desk at the Federal Reserve Bank of New York purchases a security in the open market, Federal Reserve assets increase by the value of the security purchased. A corresponding increase is recorded on the liability side of the Federal Reserve's balance sheet to reflect payment for the security; the liability item "deposits of depository institutions" rises when the account that the seller's depository institution holds at the Federal Reserve is credited.

Simplified view of the Federal Reserve balance sheet, as of January 20, 2016

The Federal Reserve publishes data weekly regarding its balance sheet.

Assets (millions of dollars)		Liabilities (millions of dollars)	
Treasury securities held outright	2,461,396	Federal Reserve notes in circulation	1,369,051
Agency debt and mortgage-backed securities holdings	1,750,275	Deposits of depository institutions	2,412,078
Other assets	277,169	Capital and other liabilities	707,711
Total	**4,488,840**	**Total**	**4,488,840**

Note: More detailed information on the balance sheet is available on the Federal Reserve Board's website, www.federalreserve.gov/monetarypolicy/bst.htm. The H.4.1 statistical release, "Factors Affecting Reserve Balances," is published every Thursday at www.federalreserve.gov/releases/h41/.

Promoting Financial System Stability

The Federal Reserve monitors financial system risks and engages at home and abroad to help ensure the system supports a healthy economy for U.S. households, communities, and businesses.

The Federal Reserve was created in 1913 to promote greater financial stability and help avoid banking panics like those that had plunged the country into deep economic contractions in the late nineteenth and early twentieth centuries.

Over the past century, as the U.S. and global financial system have evolved, the Federal Reserve's role in promoting financial stability has necessarily changed with it. The 2007–09 financial crisis and the subsequent deep recession revealed shortcomings in the financial system infrastructure and the framework for supervising and regulating it (see figure 4.1). Indeed, reforms enacted under the Dodd-Frank Wall Street Reform and Consumer Protection Act of 2010 assigned the Federal Reserve new responsibilities in the effort to promote financial system stability and keep pace with changing dynamics and innovation in the broader economy.

Figure 4.1. The financial system: key participants and linkages

Key participants in the U.S. and global financial system include the lenders and savers who are matched up with borrowers and spenders through various markets and intermediaries. The Federal Reserve monitors the financial system to ensure the linkages among these three entities are well-functioning and adjusts its policymaking or engagement with other policymakers to address any emerging concerns.

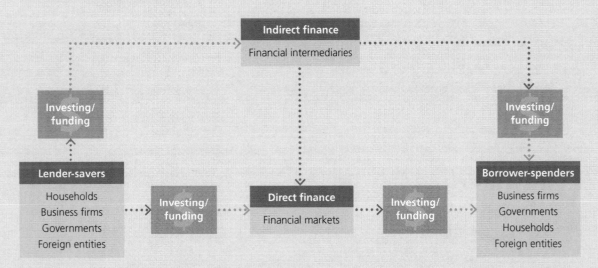

Source: Adapted from Frederic S. Mishkin and Stanley G. Eakins, *Financial Markets and Institutions*, 7th Edition (Boston: Prentice Hall, 2012), 16.

What Is Financial Stability?

A financial system is considered stable when financial institutions—banks, savings and loans, and other financial product and service providers—and financial markets are able to provide households, communities, and businesses with the resources, services, and products they need to invest, grow, and participate in a well-functioning economy.

These resources and services include

- business lines of credit, mortgages, student loans, and the other critical offerings of a sophisticated financial system; and

- savings accounts, brokerage services, and retirement accounts, among many others.

Effective Linking of Savers and Investors with Borrowers and Businesses

A healthy and stable financial system links, at the lowest possible cost, savers and investors seeking to grow their money with borrowers and businesses in need of funds. If this critical role of intermediation between savers and borrowers is disrupted in times of stress, the adverse impact will be felt across the economy.

And such disruption can carry a very high price. As a result, financial stability in its most basic form could be thought of as a condition where financial institutions and markets are able to support consumers, communities, and businesses even in an otherwise stressed economic environment.

Keeping Institutions and Market Structures Resilient

To support financial stability, it is critical that financial institutions and market structures are resilient, so that they are able to bend but not

Box 4.1. Financial Stability and the Founding of the Federal Reserve

Financial stability considerations were a key element in the founding of the Federal Reserve System. Indeed, it was created in response to the Panic of 1907, which was at the time the latest in a series of severe financial panics that befell the nation in the late nineteenth and early twentieth centuries.

The 1907 panic led to the creation of the National Monetary Commission, whose 1911 report was a major impetus to the Federal Reserve Act, signed into law by President Woodrow Wilson on December 23, 1913. Upon enactment, the process of organizing and opening the Board and the Reserve Banks across the country began. On November 16, 1914, the Federal Reserve System began full-fledged operations.

In the words of one Federal Reserve Act author, U.S. Senator Robert Latham Owen of Oklahoma, "It should always be kept in mind that . . . it is the prevention of panic, the protection of our commerce, the stability of business conditions, and the maintenance in active operation of the productive energies of the nation which is the question of vital importance."

For more information on the Federal Reserve founding, see *The Federal Reserve Act: Its Origin and Principles*, available on the Federal Reserve Bank of St. Louis website (https://fraser. stlouisfed.org/docs/publications/books/ fra_owen_1919.pdf).

break under extreme economic pressures. Such a dynamic does not mean that market prices will never rise or fall quickly. Volatility may reflect changes in economic conditions and would be a concern with respect to financial stability only when institutions and markets are not adequately prepared. Financial stability depends on firms and critical financial market structures having the financial strength and operational skills to manage through volatility and continue to provide their essential products and services to consumers, communities, and other businesses.

Monitoring Risk across the Financial System

The Federal Reserve and other bank regulators have long supervised individual banks and financial institutions to make sure they are run in a "prudent" and "safe and sound" manner and are not taking excessive risks. The goal of this traditional "microprudential" supervisory approach is to ensure individual banks and financial institutions are less likely to fail and to help avoid any associated adverse circumstances for their customers.

In the heat of the 2007–09 financial crisis, however, it became clear this microprudential focus did not adequately identify risks that developed *across and between* markets and institutions and that, in turn, threatened to set off a cascade of failures that could have undermined the entire financial system. Thus, a central element of the Dodd-Frank Act—the landmark legislative response to the 2007–09 crisis—is the requirement that the Federal Reserve and other financial regulatory agencies look across the entire financial system for risks, adopting a macroprudential approach to supervision and regulation.

Whereas a traditional—or microprudential—approach to supervision and regulation focuses on the safety and soundness of individual institutions, the macroprudential approach centers on the stability of the financial system as a whole (see section 5, "Supervising and Regulating Financial Institutions and Activities," on page 72, for more on micro- and macroprudential supervision).

Types of Financial System Vulnerabilities and Risks

Federal Reserve staff regularly and systematically assess a standard set of vulnerabilities as part of a Federal Reserve System macroprudential financial stability review:

- asset valuations and risk appetite
- leverage in the financial system
- liquidity risks and maturity transformation by the financial system
- borrowing by the nonfinancial sector (households and nonfinancial businesses)

These vulnerability assessments inform internal Federal Reserve discussions concerning both macroprudential supervision and regulatory

Microprudential supervision and regulation

The Federal Reserve also "microprudentially" supervises and regulates the operations of large financial institutions—that is, it monitors the safety and soundness of these and other individual institutions—and integrates this monitoring into its macroprudential supervisory and regulatory efforts.

For more information, see section 5, "Supervising and Regulating Financial Institutions and Activities," on page 72.

Figure 4.2. Four standard components of financial system vulnerability review

Four vulnerability assessments inform the broad efforts undertaken by the Federal Reserve—with entities both in the United States and abroad—to monitor financial system stability.

Asset valuations and risk appetites	Financial system leverage	Liquidity risks/maturity transformation	Nonfinancial sector borrowing
The "unwinding" of high prices of assets (e.g., housing prices in the mid-2000s) can destabilize the financial system and the economy	Financial system intermediaries (such as traditional banks, insurance companies, and hedge funds) with significantly more debt than equity can amplify an economic downturn	Traditional banks, money market funds, and exchange-traded funds are among the institutions that might experience a "run" by investors that amplifies an economic downturn	If credit exposure in U.S. households and nonfinancial businesses is high, these borrowers often curtail spending and disengage from other economic activity and may contribute to a severe downturn

Source: Tobias Adrian, Daniel Covitz, and Nellie Liang, "Financial Stability Monitoring," Finance and Economics Discussion Series 2013-21 (Washington: Board of Governors of the Federal Reserve System, 2013), www.federalreserve.gov/pubs/feds/2013/201321/201321pap.pdf.

policies and monetary policy (see figure 4.2). They also inform Federal Reserve interactions with broader monitoring efforts, such as those by the Financial Stability Oversight Council (FSOC) and the Financial Stability Board.

Asset Valuations and Risk Appetite

Overvalued assets constitute a fundamental vulnerability because the unwinding of high prices can be destabilizing in the financial system and economy, especially if the assets are widely held and the values are supported by excessive leverage, maturity transformation, or risk opacity. Moreover, stretched asset valuations may be an indicator of a broader buildup in risk-taking.

However, it is very difficult to judge whether an asset price is overvalued relative to fundamentals. As a result, analysis typically considers a range of possible valuation metrics, developments in areas where asset prices are rising especially rapidly or into which investor flows have been considerable, or the implications of unusually low or high levels of volatility in certain markets.

Figure 4.3. Monitoring leverage in the financial system

The collective financial strength of the banking sector—and its prevailing activities—can be an important indicator in understanding risks to the nation's financial stability. The Federal Reserve focuses on metrics like the ratio of common equity to risk-weighted assets in the banking sector, which has risen in recent years as a reflection of tougher capital standards for major banking institutions.

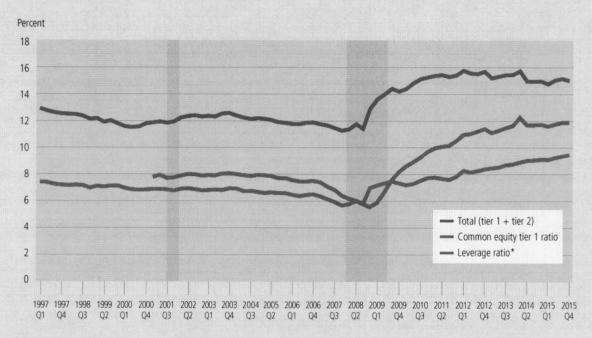

Note: Prior to 2014:Q1, the numerator of the common equity tier 1 ratio is tier 1 common capital. Beginning in 2014:Q1 for advanced-approaches bank holding companies (BHCs) and in 2015:Q1 for all other BHCs, the numerator is common equity tier 1 capital. The data for the common equity tier 1 ratio start in 2001:Q1. An advanced-approaches BHC is defined as a large internationally active banking organization, generally with at least $250 billion in total consolidated assets or at least $10 billion in total on-balance-sheet foreign exposure. The shaded bars indicate periods of business recession as defined by the National Bureau of Economic Research.

* Leverage ratio is the ratio of tier 1 capital to total assets.

Source: Federal Reserve Board, FR Y-9C, Consolidated Financial Statements for Holding Companies.

Leverage in the Financial System

Highly leveraged financial system intermediaries—those with significantly more debt than equity—can amplify the effect of negative shocks in the financial system and broad economy (see figure 4.3).

For example, if a highly leveraged institution needs to shrink its balance sheet in response to an otherwise standard economic downturn, the resulting contraction in credit will have broader economic implications. Moreover, sufficiently large losses for highly leveraged institutions can lead to "fire sales," where assets are unloaded quickly at extremely low prices. Fire sales, in turn, increase the potential for runs on banks—and even on nonbanks—if liabilities have short maturities.

The Federal Reserve monitors leverage in the banking sector with the help of an extensive data collection program. Nevertheless, these monitoring efforts are complicated by off-balance-sheet exposures and rapidly changing trading exposures. Monitoring leverage in the nonbank sector (hedge funds, for example) proves even more difficult, but periodic surveys of the providers of leverage through the Senior Credit Officer Opinion Survey (SCOOS) offers valuable insights.

Liquidity Risks and Maturity Transformation by the Financial System

One key benefit provided by the financial system is to transform short-maturity (or liquid) liabilities into long-maturity (illiquid) assets. This function is done primarily through the traditional banking system or other depository institutions, but it also occurs outside the banking system, for example, through money market mutual funds.

Liquidity and maturity transformation is productive in the sense that it allows investment projects to be funded with long-term financing while still satisfying the liquidity needs of lenders. However, the experience of the 2007–09 financial crisis demonstrated that liquidity and maturity transformation introduces systemic vulnerabilities that can threaten the broader economy (see box 4.2, "Responding to Financial System Emergencies: The Lender of Last Resort Concept in Central Banking").

When a systemwide shock results in all lenders demanding liquidity at the same time, institutions engaged in this maturity transformation are at risk of being run. Deposit insurance provides protection within the traditional banking system. Nevertheless, some assets such as repurchase agreements (or "repos"), asset-backed commercial paper (ABCP), or money market funds are also subject to run risk and, indeed, came under considerable pressure during the crisis. For this reason, the Federal Reserve actively monitors, as best it can given available data and

Monitoring leverage in the nonbank sector

The Federal Reserve's quarterly Senior Credit Officer Opinion Survey on Dealer Financing Terms (SCOOS) provides information about the availability and terms of credit in securities financing and over-the-counter derivatives markets. See "Data Releases" in the Economic Research & Data section of the Federal Reserve Board's website (www.federalreserve. gov/econresdata/releases/scoos.htm).

Figure 4.4. Monitoring borrowing in the nonfinancial sector

Borrowing by households and nonfinancial sector businesses can also influence financial stability. The Federal Reserve focuses on metrics like the ratio of household and nonfinancial business credit to nominal U.S. gross domestic product. This ratio dropped below peaks around the time of the 2007–09 crisis.

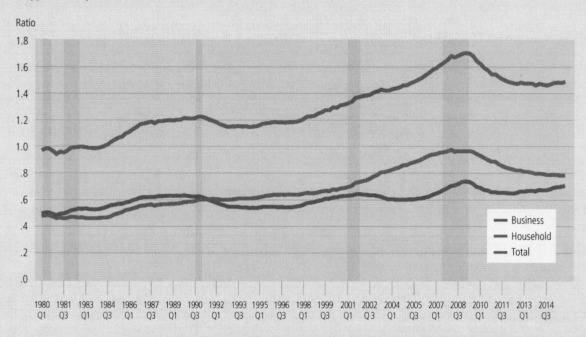

Note: The shaded bars indicate periods of business recession as defined by the National Bureau of Economic Research.

Source: Federal Reserve Board, Statistical Release Z.1, "Financial Accounts of the United States."

measurement, both liquidity risk and the degree of maturity transformation in the financial system.

Borrowing by the Nonfinancial Sector

Excessive credit in the private nonfinancial sector can provide a transmission channel for a disruption in financial markets to affect the real economy (see figure 4.4). Highly indebted households and nonfinancial businesses may have a difficult time withstanding negative shocks to incomes or asset values, and may be forced to curtail spending in ways that amplify the effects of financial shocks. In turn, losses among households and businesses can lead to mounting losses at financial institutions, creating an adverse feedback loop. The Federal Reserve monitors measures of vulnerabilities in the nonfinancial sector including, for example, leverage and debt service burdens as well as underwriting standards on new loans to households and businesses.

This monitoring program is complemented by a broader effort to foster greater transparency in financial markets through improved data collection and enhanced disclosures by regulated financial market participants. Greater transparency helps lead to meaningful implementation of macroprudential regulatory and supervisory policies to target building vulnerabilities and to pre-position the financial system to be better able to absorb shocks.

Why Proactive Monitoring of Domestic and Foreign Markets Matters

The changing nature of risks and fluctuations in financial markets and the broader economy require timely monitoring of the effects of conditions in domestic and foreign financial markets on financial institutions and even in the nonfinancial sector in order to identify the buildup of vulnerabilities that might require further study or policy action.

Financial stability policy and research

The Federal Reserve works to identify threats to financial stability and develop effective policies to address those threats through its Division of Financial Stability. This office monitors financial markets, institutions, and structures and also conducts research on financial stability issues. For more information, see the complete list of Federal Reserve Board working papers (www.federalreserve.gov/econresdata/workingpapers.htm).

To this end, the Federal Reserve maintains a flexible, forward-looking financial stability monitoring program to help inform policymakers of the financial system's vulnerabilities to a range of potential adverse events or shocks. Such a monitoring program is a critical part of a broader Federal Reserve System effort to assess and address vulnerabilities in the U.S. financial system. In the case of individual institutions, the Federal Reserve may take more direct action and in various ways (for more information, see "Macroprudential Supervision and Monitoring" on page 98 in section 5, "Supervising and Regulating Financial Institutions and Activities").

Examining Causes, Effects, and Remedies for Financial Instability

A macroprudential approach to ensuring financial stability builds on a substantial and growing body of research on the factors that lead to

Box 4.2. Responding to Financial System Emergencies: The Lender of Last Resort Concept in Central Banking

The idea that a central bank should provide liquidity to support the financial system was refined by nineteenth-century economist Walter Bagehot, who suggested that during times of financial panic or crisis, a central bank should lend quickly and freely, at a penalty rate of interest, to any borrower with good collateral.

When a major shock—like a natural disaster, a terrorist attack, or a financial panic—occurs that severely stresses the financial system, people, businesses, and financial institutions need access to money and credit. Indeed, having this liquidity available can improve confidence in the economy and restore calm to markets, bolstering the stability of the financial system.

General authority during times of crisis. To provide liquidity during times of crisis, the Federal Reserve—like many central banks—is empowered to function as a "lender of last resort" (LOLR), and it uses different tools to fulfill this role.

In an emergency, the Federal Reserve has the power to provide liquidity to depository institutions using standard, traditional tools, like open market operations and discount window lending. Under section 13(3) of the Federal Reserve Act, the U.S. central bank also has authority to provide liquidity to nondepository institutions in "unusual and exigent circumstances." Although the Federal Reserve has rarely exercised this LOLR clause enacted in 1932, it did use it during the 2007–09 financial crisis to prevent harm to the U.S. economy.

Broad-based lending only. Under amendments enacted under the

Dodd-Frank Act, emergency lending programs under section 13(3) of the Federal Reserve Act must be broad-based and not designed to support a single institution, among other requirements. In addition, Congress requires that the Federal Reserve ensure that taxpayers are protected against losses.

For a fuller discussion of how each of these lending tools works, see section 3, "Conducting Monetary Policy," on page 20 (see also the 2013 Federal Reserve paper "Financial Stability Monitoring," www.federalreserve.gov/pubs/feds/2013/201321/201321pap.pdf).

Federal Reserve lending under normal and "unusual and exigent" circumstances

As a major financial crisis began to unfold in 2007 and its magnitude became clearer, the Federal Reserve invoked its statutory authority to lend to qualified institutions with adequate collateral. At its peak, Federal Reserve credit outstanding reached more than $1.2 trillion—but within four years it had abated to near pre-crisis levels as economic and financial conditions improved.

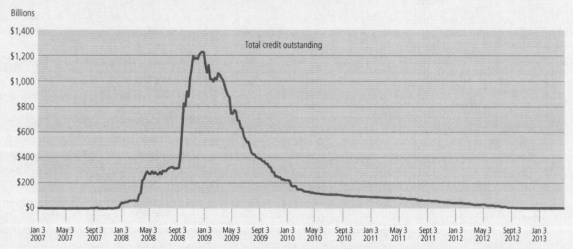

Billions

Source: Federal Reserve H.4.1 Statistical Release, Table 1. Factors Affecting Reserve Balances of Depository Institutions and Condition Statement of Federal Reserve Banks. See the Economic Research & Data section of the Federal Reserve Board's website, www.federalreserve.gov.

vulnerabilities in the financial system and how government policies can mitigate such risks.

The Federal Reserve actively engages in financial stability research to improve understanding of issues related to financial stability and to engage with the broader research community on crucial policy matters. This engagement often involves collaboration with researchers at other domestic and international institutions.

Macroprudential Supervision and Regulation of Large, Complex Financial Institutions

Large, complex financial institutions interact with financial markets and the broader economy in a manner that may—during times of stress and in the absence of an appropriate regulatory framework and effective supervision—lead to financial instability. The Federal Reserve promotes the safety and soundness of these institutions through robust supervision and regulation programs, two components of which are integral to its macroprudential efforts.

Types of systemically important financial institutions

Visit the Financial Stability Oversight Council website at www.treasury.gov/initiatives/fsoc/designations for a discussion of systemically important institutions.

Monitoring Systemically Important Financial Institutions

The macroprudential approach informs Federal Reserve supervision of systemically important financial institutions (SIFIs)—including large bank holding companies (BHCs), the U.S. operations of certain foreign banking organizations (FBOs), and financial market utilities (FMUs). In addition, the Federal Reserve serves as a "consolidated supervisor" of nonbank financial companies that the FSOC has determined should be supervised by the Federal Reserve Board and subject to prudential standards. (See "Domestic and International Cooperation and Coordination" on page 68 for more information on the FSOC.)

The Federal Reserve actively monitors indicators of the riskiness of SIFIs, both individually as well as through interlinkages in the broader network of financial institutions, to help identify vulnerabilities. It also imposes certain regulatory requirements on SIFIs in order to limit potentially risky activities by these institutions and to mitigate spillover of distress into the broader economy. If a SIFI were to become distressed, disruptions in the financial system could arise from direct losses imposed on SIFI counterparties, contagion, fire sales effects, or a loss of critical services.

SIFIs are also subject to additional capital and liquidity regulations imposed by the Federal Reserve in order to help mitigate some of the additional risks they pose to the financial system as a whole, given their size and interconnectedness.

Moreover, during the 2007–09 financial crisis, the lack of effective resolution strategies contributed to the pernicious spillovers of distress at or between individual institutions and from those institutions to the broader economy. The Federal Reserve, in collaboration with other U.S. agencies, has continued to work with large financial institutions to develop a range of recovery and resolution strategies in the event of their distress or failure. Improvements in resolution planning are intended to, among other things, mitigate adverse effects from perceptions of "too big to fail" and contribute to more orderly conditions in the financial system if institutions face strains or fail. (For more information on recovery and resolution planning activity, see section 5, "Supervising and Regulating Financial Institutions and Activities," on page 72.)

Stress Testing of Key Financial Institutions

One important element of enhanced supervision of SIFIs is the stress-testing process, which includes the Dodd-Frank Act stress tests and the

Comprehensive Capital Analysis and Review. In addition to fostering the safety and soundness of the participating institutions, the stress test program includes macroprudential elements such as

"Stress testing" of large financial institutions

In 2015, 31 institutions participated in the Federal Reserve stress testing process, which occurs annually. For more information, see the "Stress Tests and Capital Planning" web page, located on the Banking Information & Regulation section of the Federal Reserve Board's website (www.federalreserve. gov/bankinforeg/stress-tests-capital-planning.htm).

- examination of the loss-absorbing capacity of institutions under a common macroeconomic scenario that has features similar to the strains experienced in a severe recession and which includes, as appropriate, identified salient risks;

- conducting horizontal testing across large institutions to understand the potential correlated exposures; and

- consideration of the effects of counterparty distress on the largest, most interconnected firms.

The macroeconomic and financial scenarios that are used in the stress tests have proved to be an important macroprudential tool. The Federal Reserve adjusts the severity of the macroeconomic scenario used in the stress tests in a way that counteracts the natural tendency for risks to build within the financial system during periods of strong economic activity. The scenarios can also be used to assess the financial system's vulnerability to particularly significant risks and to highlight certain risks to institutions participating in the testing.

Intersection of Financial Stability and Monetary Policy

Promotion of financial stability strongly complements the primary goals of monetary policy—maximum employment and price stability. A smoothly operating financial system promotes the efficient allocation of saving and investment, facilitating economic growth and employment. And price stability contributes not only to the efficient allocation of resources in the real economy (that is, the part of the economy that produces goods and services), but also to reduced uncertainty and efficient pricing in financial markets that, in turn, supports financial stability.

Domestic and International Cooperation and Coordination

Economic and financial volatility in any country can have negative consequences for the world, but sizable and significant spillovers are almost assured from an economy that is large.

In its role promoting financial stability, the Federal Reserve cooperates and coordinates with many other domestic and international regulatory and policy entities. The FSOC is an important forum for cooperation with other domestic agencies (see figure 4.5). The primary venues for international cooperation occur through the Basel Committee on Banking Supervision and the Financial Stability Board.

Domestic Engagement through the Financial Stability Oversight Council

The FSOC, created in 2010 under the Dodd-Frank Act and chaired by the U.S. Treasury Secretary, draws on the expertise of the Federal Reserve and other regulators to proactively identify risks to financial stability, promote market discipline, and respond to emerging threats. The Chair of the Federal Reserve is a member of the FSOC, and the Federal Reserve works to support the activities of the FSOC and other U.S. government agencies in the pursuit of financial stability.

Through collaborative participation in the FSOC, U.S. financial regulators monitor not only institutions but the financial system as a whole. The Federal Reserve plays an important role in this macroprudential framework: it assists in monitoring financial risks, analyzes the implications of those risks for financial stability, and identifies steps that can be taken to mitigate those risks.

Central banks around the world

The central bank concept dates to 1668 when Sweden's Riksbank was formed.

As of December 2015, there were 178 central banks and monetary authorities around the world, and the Federal Reserve interacts with many of them in its efforts to promote financial stability in the U.S. and global economies.

See www.bis.org/cbanks.htm for a listing of central banks.

Regular reporting on FSOC activities

The Financial Stability Oversight Council (FSOC) meets routinely to coordinate on financial stability topics that might affect the U.S. economy and publishes both its monthly meeting minutes and annual report. For more information, see the FSOC website (www.treasury.gov/initiatives/fsoc/pages/home.aspx).

Figure 4.5. The framework for monitoring U.S. financial system stability

The Financial Stability Oversight Council, a blend of federal and state regulators, meets routinely to coordinate on financial stability topics that might affect the U.S. economy and makes publicly available its meeting minutes, annual report, and various other studies and statements. For more information, see the FSOC website (www.treasury.gov/initiatives/fsoc/pages/home.aspx).

[1] Non-voting member serves two-year term.

[2] Non-voting member.

Figure 4.6. Monitoring financial system stability requires global cooperation

What happens in the global economy can influence—sometimes greatly—the stability of the U.S. economy. Because the U.S. dollar is a widely used global currency and because the world's economies are interdependent, the Federal Reserve works closely with central banks and other public authorities around the world to address international financial issues and promote financial stability.

International authority/ deliberative body	Overview/Federal Reserve engagement
Central banks Established: 1668 or later Location: Throughout the world Website: www.bis.org/central_bank_hub_overview.htm	Nearly all developed and developing nations maintain central banks to promote a sound and stable financial system and well-functioning economies. Indeed, Federal Reserve officials engage regularly and collectively with other central banks to discuss broad trends affecting the global financial system; one-on-one bank engagement also occurs in special circumstances where coordination and cooperation can help keep the global financial system operating smoothly.
Bank of International Settlements Established: 1930 Location: Basel, Switzerland Website: www.bis.org	The Bank of International Settlements seeks, among other things, to foster discussion and facilitate collaboration among central banks and supports dialogue with other authorities that are responsible for promoting financial stability. The Federal Reserve participates in the deliberations of this financial organization, whose members include 60 member central banks, representing countries from around the world that together make up about 95 percent of world gross domestic product.
Financial Stability Board Established: 2009 Location: Basel, Switzerland Website: www.fsb.org	The Financial Stability Board (FSB), successor to the Financial Stability Forum, promotes stability in the international financial system through enhanced cooperation among various national and international supervisory bodies and international financial institutions. The Federal Reserve Board and other U.S. agencies participate in FSB efforts, which specifically seek to coordinate the development of regulatory, supervisory, and other financial sector policies.
G7 & G20 Established: 1975 (as G6) Location: Varies by nation hosting Website: Varies by nation hosting	The Group of Seven (G7) is an informal bloc of industrialized democracies (also including Canada, France, Germany, Italy, Japan, and the United Kingdom) that meets annually to discuss global economic issues. Federal Reserve officials engage regularly with the G7 and G20 to discuss macroeconomic policy surveillance, the international financial system, and a wide range of policy issues such as development and policy proposals to encourage strong, sustainable, and balanced growth.
International Monetary Fund Established: 1945 Location: Washington, DC Website: www.imf.org	The International Monetary Fund (IMF) works to "foster global monetary cooperation, secure financial stability, facilitate international trade, promote high employment and sustainable economic growth, and reduce poverty around the world." The Federal Reserve is a member of the International Monetary and Financial Committee, which advises and reports to the IMF Board of Governors on the supervision and management of the international monetary and financial system, including on responses to unfolding events that may disrupt the system.
Organisation for Economic Co-operation and Development Established: 1961 Location: Paris, France Website: www.oecd.org	The Organisation for Economic Co-operation and Development (OECD) promotes "policies that will improve the economic and social well-being of people around the world." The Federal Reserve participates in several OECD forums to discuss current economic issues and projections for the global economic outlook, and to promote policies that will improve global economic well-being.
World Bank Established: 1944 Location: Washington, DC Website: www.worldbank.org	The World Bank functions as a cooperative of 189 member countries. These member countries, or shareholders, are represented by a board of governors, who are the ultimate policymakers at the World Bank. Generally, the governors are member countries' ministers of finance or ministers of development. The Federal Reserve interacts informally with the World Bank, largely through the International Monetary Fund.

Engagement with Regulatory Authorities Abroad

The Federal Reserve participates in international bodies, such as the Basel Committee on Banking Supervision and the Financial Stability Board, to address issues associated with the interconnected global financial system and the global activities of large U.S. financial institutions (see figure 4.6).

Through both venues, the Federal Reserve is engaged with the international community in monitoring the global financial system and promoting the adoption of sound policies across countries.

Supervising and Regulating Financial Institutions and Activities

The Federal Reserve promotes the safety and soundness of individual financial institutions and monitors their impact on the financial system as a whole.

5

The Federal Reserve Act of 1913 established the Federal Reserve System to provide the nation with a safer, more flexible, and more stable monetary and financial system. One of the principal functions of the Federal Reserve in achieving this goal is to regulate and supervise various financial entities. It performs this function, in part, through microprudential regulation and supervision of banks; holding companies and their affiliates; and other entities, including nonbank financial companies that the Financial Stability Oversight Council (FSOC) has determined should be supervised by the Board and subject to prudential standards. In addition, the Federal Reserve engages in "macroprudential" supervision and regulation that looks beyond the safety and soundness of individual institutions to promote the stability of the financial system as a whole.

Figure 5.1. How the regulation and supervision process works

When Congress passes a law that impacts the financial industry, the Federal Reserve—sometimes in cooperation with other federal agencies—often drafts regulations that determine how the law will be implemented.

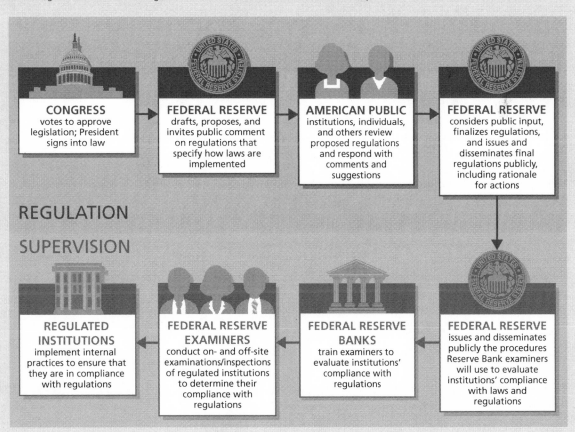

Regulation versus Supervision

Regulation and supervision are distinct, but complementary, activities (see figure 5.1). Regulation entails establishing the rules within which financial institutions must operate—in other words, issuing specific regulations and guidelines governing the formation, operations, activities, and acquisitions of financial institutions. Once the rules and regulations are established, supervision—which involves monitoring, inspecting, and examining financial institutions—seeks to ensure that an institution complies with those rules and regulations, and that it operates in a safe and sound manner.

Entities the Federal Reserve Oversees

By law, the Federal Reserve is responsible for supervising and regulating certain segments of the financial industry to ensure they employ safe and sound business practices and comply with all applicable laws and regulations (see figure 5.2).

Bank Holding Companies (Including Financial Holding Companies)

Banks are often owned or controlled by another company, called a bank holding company (BHC). The Federal Reserve has supervisory and regulatory authority for all BHCs, regardless of whether subsidiary banks of the holding company are national banks, state "member" banks, or state "nonmember" banks (see a complete discussion of "State Member Banks" beginning on page 77). It also has supervisory authority over any nonbank subsidiary of a BHC that is not functionally regulated by another federal or state regulator, such as a leasing subsidiary.

The Gramm-Leach-Bliley Act of 1999 permits BHCs that meet certain criteria to become financial holding companies (also under Federal Reserve supervisory and regulatory authority). These entities may own

Figure 5.2. The Federal Reserve oversees a broad range of financial entities

Bank holding companies constitute the largest segment of institutions supervised by the Federal Reserve, but the Federal Reserve also supervises state member banks, savings and loan holding companies, foreign banks operating in the United States, and other entities.

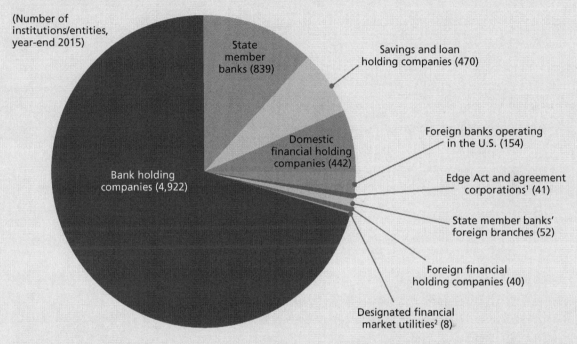

(Number of institutions/entities, year-end 2015)

- Bank holding companies (4,922)
- State member banks (839)
- Savings and loan holding companies (470)
- Domestic financial holding companies (442)
- Foreign banks operating in the U.S. (154)
- Edge Act and agreement corporations[1] (41)
- State member banks' foreign branches (52)
- Foreign financial holding companies (40)
- Designated financial market utilities[2] (8)

[1] Edge Act and agreement corporations are subsidiaries of banks or bank holding companies, organized to allow international banking and financial business.

[2] Financial market utilities (FMUs) are multilateral systems that provide the essential infrastructure for transferring, clearing, and settling payments, securities, and other financial transactions among financial institutions or between financial institutions and within those systems. The Federal Reserve supervises FMUs, including certain ones that have been designated systemically important by the Financial Stability Oversight Council.

Note: Entities supervised are not mutually exclusive; for example, bank and savings and loan holding companies may own other supervised entities listed.

Source: *2015 Annual Report*, "Supervision and Regulation" (available on the Federal Reserve Board's website, www.federalreserve.gov/publications/annual-report/2015-supervision-and-regulation.htm).

(1) broker-dealers engaged in securities underwriting and dealing and (2) business entities engaged in merchant banking, insurance underwriting, and insurance agency activities.

When a financial holding company owns a subsidiary broker-dealer or insurance company, the Federal Reserve coordinates its supervisory efforts with those of the subsidiary's functional regulator—for example, the U.S.

Securities and Exchange Commission (SEC) in the case of a broker-dealer, and state insurance regulators in the case of an insurance company.

For a current list of financial holding companies, visit the Banking Information & Regulation section of the Federal Reserve Board's website (Banking Structure section), at www.federalreserve.gov.

Savings and Loan Holding Companies

Savings and loan holding companies directly or indirectly control either a savings association or other savings and loan holding companies. Federal savings associations (those with federal charters) are supervised by the Office of the Comptroller of the Currency (OCC) while state-chartered savings associations are generally supervised by the Federal Deposit Insurance Corporation (FDIC) and their chartering state. Besides owning federal and/or state savings associations, a savings and loan holding company that meets capital and management requirements and elects to be treated as a financial holding company may also (1) operate as or own a broker-dealer engaged in securities underwriting and dealing, (2) engage in merchant banking, and (3) operate as or own an insurance company.

Historically, savings and loan holding companies were regulated by other agencies: at first, the Federal Home Loan Bank Board, and more recently, by the Office of Thrift Supervision (OTS). In 2010, the Dodd-Frank Wall Street Reform and Consumer Protection Act (Dodd-Frank Act) transferred supervisory and regulatory responsibilities for savings and loan holding companies from the now-defunct OTS to the Federal Reserve.

As a result, the Federal Reserve now supervises and regulates all savings and loan holding companies regardless of the charters of the subsidiary savings associations. The Federal Reserve coordinates its supervisory efforts with the appropriate functional regulator(s) for a savings and loan holding company that owns or operates as a broker-dealer or insurance company.

Bank charters affect their supervision

The current U.S. supervisory system for banks, in which an institution may be either federally or state-chartered, and may belong to the Federal Reserve System or not, has evolved historically. The Federal Reserve shares supervisory and regulatory responsibility for domestic banks with other federal regulators and with individual state banking departments.

State Member Banks

The Federal Reserve is the primary federal supervisor of state-chartered banks that have chosen to join the Federal Reserve System. Such domestically operating banks are called "state member banks."

The Federal Reserve shares supervisory and regulatory responsibility for domestic banks with the OCC and the FDIC at the federal level, and with individual state banking departments at the state level.

Figure 5.3. Oversight of the financial industry is shared among federal regulators

The primary supervisor of a domestic banking organization is generally determined by the type of institution it is and the governmental authority that granted it permission to commence business.

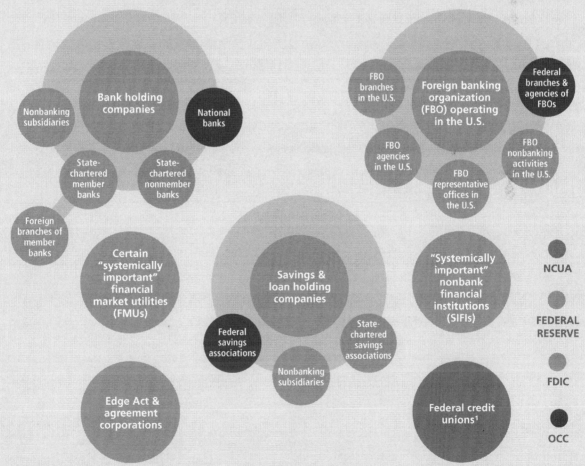

Note: Figure 5.3 focuses on the federal banking regulators. Other federal regulators oversee the financial industry as well, including the Securities and Exchange Commission, the Commodities Futures Trading Commission, and the Consumer Financial Protection Bureau, among others.

[1] Federal credit unions are not considered part of the banking industry, but offer similar if more limited services than banks.

The primary federal supervisor of a domestic bank (see figure 5.3) is generally determined by two key factors: (1) whether the bank chooses to operate under a federal or state charter and (2) the governmental authority (federal or state) that then grants it permission to commence business operations.

Banks chartered by a state government entity are referred to as state banks; banks that are chartered by the OCC, an independent bureau of the U.S. Department of the Treasury, are referred to as national banks.

State banks that are not members of the Federal Reserve System (collectively referred to as "state nonmember banks") are supervised by the FDIC. In addition to being supervised by the Federal Reserve or the FDIC, state banks are also supervised by their chartering state. In contrast, the OCC supervises national banks that choose to charter at the federal level.

Edge Act and Agreement Corporations

Edge Act and agreement corporations are U.S. financial institutions that carry out international banking and financing operations, some of which the parent banks themselves are not permitted to undertake under existing laws. These corporations, which are examined annually, may act as holding companies, provide international banking services, and finance industrial and financial projects abroad, among other activities.

Financial Market Utilities

Financial market utilities (FMUs) and financial institutions participating in payment, clearance, and settlement (PCS) activities comprise the nation's financial infrastructure. This infrastructure supports millions of financial transactions every day and encompasses many transactional elements: small-value retail payment systems (such as credit card and debit card networks) and large-value PCS systems for financial transactions, including central counterparties, foreign-exchange settlement systems, and large-dollar funds transfer systems. The smooth and reliable functioning of this financial infrastructure at all times is vitally important to the stability of the financial system and the health of the broader economy.

Because their operations are so vital, FMUs can contribute to systemic risk. In other words, problems at one system or institution could spill over to other systems or financial institutions in the form of liquidity or credit disruptions—particularly since FMUs have become increasingly interdependent. For example, today, fewer and larger utilities (such as clearinghouses) support more integrated markets and global financial firms. Moreover, the same large banks participate in all of the major clearinghouses, and the major clearinghouses often rely on similar sets of banks for payment services, funding, settlement, and emergency liquidity. In this environment, problems at one clearinghouse could have significant effects on others, even in the absence of explicit operational links.

For more information on regulation and supervision of the payment and settlement system, see "Regulating and Supervising the Payment System" on page 142.

Nonbank Financial Companies

The Dodd-Frank Act assigned the Federal Reserve the authority and responsibility to supervise and regulate certain nonbank financial companies that the FSOC has determined should be subject to Board supervision and prudential standards pursuant to section 113 of that act.

These firms—whose failure could pose a threat to U.S. financial stability—are subject to comprehensive, consolidated supervision and regulation by the Federal Reserve. This provision of the Dodd-Frank Act addresses an important regulatory gap that existed before the 2007–09 financial crisis.

Because the material distress or failure of a nonbank financial institution supervised by the Federal Reserve can have an outsized effect on the financial sector and the real economy, the Dodd-Frank Act requires the Federal Reserve to reduce the probability of such events through

What does "systemically important" mean?

If the Financial Stability Oversight Council (FSOC) determines that a nonbank financial company's material financial distress—or the nature, scope, size, scale, concentration, interconnectedness, or mix of its activities—could pose a threat to U.S. financial stability, the company is often referred to as being "systemically important." Similarly, the FSOC may designate certain financial market utilities as systemically important.

prudential standards for nonbank financial institutions designated by the FSOC. These heightened prudential standards, stipulated in section 165 of the Dodd-Frank Act and applicable also to the largest U.S. BHCs and foreign banking organizations, become progressively more stringent as the systemic importance of that regulated entity increases and include enhanced risk-based capital and leverage requirements, liquidity requirements, overall risk-management requirements, concentration limits, resolution plan (that is, "living will") requirements, and credit exposure reporting requirements. In addition to the mandatory heightened standards, the Federal Reserve may establish additional prudential standards for designated nonbank financial companies that the Federal Reserve determines are appropriate.

The Federal Reserve's Role in the Supervision of Certain Insurance Holding Companies

The Federal Reserve assumed responsibility as the consolidated supervisor of certain insurance holding companies as a result of the Dodd-Frank Act. In addition to certain nonbank financial companies described above that may have significant insurance activities, the Federal Reserve is responsible for the consolidated supervision of insurance holding companies that are savings and loan holding companies. While the activities of insurance companies may differ from the activities of state member banks and BHCs, the Federal Reserve's principal supervisory objectives for insurance holding companies remain protecting the safety and soundness of the consolidated firms and their subsidiary depository institutions. To achieve these objectives, the Federal Reserve coordinates supervisory activities with state insurance regulators, who continue to have oversight of insurance legal entities.

Oversight Councils

Two councils—comprised of federal and state regulators and including Federal Reserve representatives—play important coordinating roles in the supervision and regulation of financial institutions.

Financial Stability Oversight Council

As noted earlier, the FSOC is a formal interagency body established by the Dodd-Frank Act. Its statutory purposes are to

- identify risks to the stability of the U.S. financial system that could arise from the distress or failure, or ongoing activities, of large, interconnected bank holding companies or nonbank financial companies or that could arise outside the financial service marketplace;

- promote market discipline by eliminating expectations on the part of the shareholders, creditors, and counterparties of such companies that the U.S. government will shield them from losses in the event of the company's failure; and

- respond to emerging threats to U.S. financial stability.

Also among its responsibilities are determining whether nonbank financial companies should be subject to Board supervision and prudential standards and designating FMUs as systemically important, as appropriate. The FSOC is also responsible for identifying and working to address gaps in regulation.

Federal Financial Institutions Examination Council (FFIEC)

The FFIEC is a formal interagency body that includes representatives of the Federal Reserve Board, the FDIC, the OCC, the Consumer Financial Protection Bureau (CFPB), the National Credit Union Administration, and the State Liaison Committee.

The FFIEC was created in 1978 to

- prescribe uniform federal principles and standards for the examination of depository institutions,

- promote coordination of supervision among the federal agencies that regulate financial institutions, and

- encourage better coordination of federal and state regulatory activities.

Through the FFIEC, state and federal regulatory agencies may exchange views on important regulatory issues. Among other things, the FFIEC has developed uniform financial reports that federally supervised banks file with their federal regulator.

How the Federal Reserve Supervises Financial Institutions

In overseeing the institutions under its authority, the Federal Reserve seeks primarily to promote their safe and sound functioning, as well as their compliance with all applicable laws and regulations that govern their activities.

Microprudential, Safety-and-Soundness Supervision

As a matter of law and practice, the Federal Reserve and other financial regulatory agencies have traditionally adhered to a microprudential approach to supervision; in other words, the regulator has focused on ensuring the health and soundness of individual financial institutions, particularly insured depository institutions (such as banks).

This approach remains a key component in Federal Reserve supervision. But, as the 2007–09 financial crisis demonstrated, the Federal Reserve and other financial regulatory agencies must also take into account

Box 5.1. Microprudential versus Macroprudential Supervision

The Federal Reserve takes a two-pronged approach to its oversight of financial institutions:

1. The **microprudential** approach seeks to ensure the safety and soundness of individual institutions and involves in-depth examinations and inspections of the structure, operations, and compliance of individual entities regulated by the Federal Reserve.

2. The **macroprudential** approach focuses on the soundness and resilience of the financial system as a whole and addresses how the actions of one institution, or set of institutions, can impact other institutions and the U.S. economic and financial system overall.

These two approaches to supervision are complementary. The financial system as a whole is more likely to be stable if its constituent organizations are sound. And traditional, firm-specific oversight provides the knowledge base for a more systemic, macroprudential approach. It is not possible to understand developments in the financial system as a whole without a clear view of developments within key firms and markets.

macroprudential risks to overall financial stability when supervising financial institutions and critical financial infrastructures. A too-narrow focus on the safety and soundness of individual banking organizations makes it harder to assess the broader financial landscape, and to detect and mitigate potential threats to financial stability that cut across many firms and markets.

Examinations and Inspections

The main objective of the Federal Reserve's longstanding microprudential supervisory process is to assess and ensure the overall safety and soundness of individual banking organizations. This evaluation includes an assessment of an organization's risk-management systems, financial condition, and compliance with applicable laws and regulations.

The supervisory process entails both on-site examinations and inspections and off-site scrutiny and monitoring. For the largest financial institutions, the Federal Reserve maintains a continuous supervisory presence, with dedicated teams of full-time examiners.

By statute, state member banks must have an on-site examination at least once every 12 months. Banks that have assets of less than $1 billion and that also meet certain management, capital, and other criteria may be examined less frequently (once every 18 months). Conversely, banks that are in troubled condition may be examined more frequently. The Federal Reserve coordinates its examinations of state member banks with those of the chartering state's bank supervisor and it may alternate examinations with the bank's state supervisor.

The objectives of an examination are, essentially, to

1. provide an objective evaluation of a bank's soundness;

2. determine the level of risk involved in the bank's transactions and activities;

3. ascertain the extent of the bank's compliance with banking laws and regulations;

4. evaluate the adequacy of the bank's corporate governance and assess the quality of its board of directors and management; and

5. identify those areas where corrective action is required to strengthen the bank, improve the quality of its performance, and enable it to comply with applicable laws, regulations, and supervisory policies and guidance.

The Federal Reserve generally conducts an annual full-scope inspection of BHCs and savings and loan holding companies with consolidated assets of $1 billion or greater, as well as smaller bank or savings and loan holding companies that have significant nonbank activities or elevated risk profiles.

In the case of small, noncomplex BHCs and savings and loan holding companies whose consolidated assets are primarily held by subsidiaries, Federal Reserve examiners rely heavily on continuous off-site monitoring and on the results of examinations of the company's subsidiary banks or savings associations by the primary federal or state authorities. This approach minimizes duplication of effort and reduces burden on smaller financial institutions.

Who conducts examinations and inspections?
Examinations and inspections are conducted by Federal Reserve examiners, professionals who work at local Federal Reserve Banks. They are rigorously trained to keep abreast of ever-evolving laws and regulations to which regulated entities are subject.

Risk-Focused Approach to Consolidated Supervision

The Federal Reserve takes a risk-focused approach to consolidated supervision, the goal of which is twofold:

1. to identify the greatest risks and emerging risks to a supervised institution; and

2. to assess the ability of the institution's management to identify, measure, monitor, and control these risks.

Consolidated supervision of holding companies encompasses the parent company and its subsidiaries, and allows the Federal Reserve to un-

Figure 5.4. Federal Reserve committee strengthens supervision of largest, most complex institutions

The Large Institution Supervision Coordinating Committee is a collaborative body providing Systemwide and cross-disciplinary perspectives on the supervision of selected large and complex domestic bank holding companies, foreign banking organizations, and nonbank financial companies.[1]

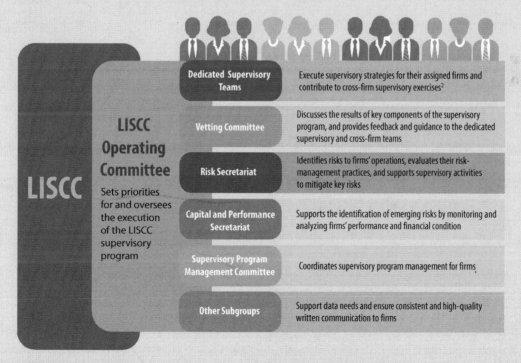

LISCC Operating Committee		
	Dedicated Supervisory Teams	Execute supervisory strategies for their assigned firms and contribute to cross-firm supervisory exercises[2]
Sets priorities for and oversees the execution of the LISCC supervisory program	**Vetting Committee**	Discusses the results of key components of the supervisory program, and provides feedback and guidance to the dedicated supervisory and cross-firm teams
	Risk Secretariat	Identifies risks to firms' operations, evaluates their risk-management practices, and supports supervisory activities to mitigate key risks
	Capital and Performance Secretariat	Supports the identification of emerging risks by monitoring and analyzing firms' performance and financial condition
	Supervisory Program Management Committee	Coordinates supervisory program management for firms
	Other Subgroups	Support data needs and ensure consistent and high-quality written communication to firms

1 For more information on the committees, subgroups, and dedicated supervisory teams that comprise the LISCC governance structure, see SR letter 15-7, Governance Structure of the LISCC Supervisory Program at www.federalreserve.gov/bankinforeg/srletters/sr1507.htm.

2 For a list of firms in the LISCC portfolio, see www.federalreserve.gov/bankinforeg/large-institution-supervision.htm.

derstand the organization's structure, activities, resources, and risks, as well as to address financial, managerial, operational, or other deficiencies before they pose a danger to the holding company's subsidiary depository institution(s). Under the risk-focused approach, Federal Reserve examiners focus on those business activities that may pose the greatest risk to the institution. For the largest financial institutions, which have grown in both size and complexity in recent years, this risk-focused approach is typically implemented through a continuous process of on-site supervision rather than through point-in-time examinations.

In 2010, to strengthen its supervision of the largest, most complex financial institutions, the Federal Reserve created a centralized multidisciplinary body called the Large Institution Supervision Coordinating Committee (LISCC) to coordinate the supervision and evaluate the conditions of these supervised institutions, which include

- domestic BHCs that have been designated as G-SIBs (global systemically important banks),
- foreign banking organizations that maintain large and complex operations in the United States, and
- nonbank financial companies that the FSOC has determined should be supervised by the Board.

The LISCC's primary functions are to provide (1) Systemwide and cross-disciplinary perspectives on the supervision of firms in the LISCC portfolio and (2) advice on the strategic direction of LISCC portfolio supervision to the Board's Director of Banking Supervision and Regulation, who serves as the Chair of the LISCC.

The LISCC Operating Committee (OC), in consultation with the LISCC, is responsible for setting priorities for and overseeing the execution of the LISCC supervisory program. The OC is a multidisciplinary group comprised of senior officials from various divisions at the Board of Governors and Reserve Banks. The OC is chaired by a senior officer from the Board's Division of Banking Supervision and Regulation who reports to the division director.

Finding reporting data on institutions supervised by the Federal Reserve

The National Information Center (www.ffiec.gov/nicpubweb/nicweb/nichome.aspx) is a repository, maintained by the Federal Financial Institutions Examination Council, that provides data about banks and other institutions, including both domestic and foreign banking organizations operating in the United States.

The OC provides direction to the LISCC firms' dedicated supervisory teams and directly oversees several subgroups, described in figure 5.4, which are collectively tasked with execution of the LISCC supervisory program.

One major supervisory exercise conducted by the LISCC each year is the Comprehensive Capital Analysis and Review (CCAR) of the largest U.S. banking firms. Building on supervisory work coming out of the crisis, CCAR was established to ensure that each of the largest U.S. BHCs maintains (1) rigorous, forward-looking capital planning processes that effectively account for the unique risks of the firm and (2) sufficient capital to continue operations throughout times of economic and financial stress.

For more information about CCAR, as well as stress testing required under the Dodd-Frank Act, see section 4, "Promoting Financial System Stability," on page 54, and "Capital Planning, Stress Testing, and Capital Distributions" on page 112.

In addition to CCAR, major annual, cross-firm supervisory exercises conducted by the LISCC include the Comprehensive Liquidity Annual Review (CLAR) and Supervisory Assessment of Recovery and Resolution Preparedness (SRP). CLAR is the Federal Reserve's program to evaluate the liquidity position and liquidity risk-management practices of LISCC firms. SRP is the Federal Reserve's review of the LISCC firms' options to support recovery and progress in removing impediments to orderly resolution. The LISCC also oversees additional cross-firm initiatives that are developed in support of LISCC priorities.

Areas and Types of Examination

The Federal Reserve examines institutions for compliance with a broad range of laws, regulations, and other legal requirements to ensure their safe and sound functioning. Further, it supervises for compliance with laws and regulations on focused topics, such as anti-money laundering and consumer protection. For more information on consumer-oriented supervision, see "Consumer-Focused Supervision and Examination" on page 154.

Financial Condition: Call Reports, the FR Y-9C, and Other Disclosures

In conducting examination programs, Federal Reserve examiners and supervisory staff rely on many sources of information about financial institutions and activities, including reports of recent examinations and inspections, public filings with the SEC, other publicly available information, and the standard financial regulatory reports filed by institutions.

The primary financial report for banks and savings associations is the Consolidated Report of Condition and Income (FFIEC 031/041), often referred to as the Call Report. It is used to prepare a Uniform Bank Performance Report, which employs ratio analysis to detect unusual or significant changes in a bank's financial condition that may warrant supervisory attention. The primary financial report for large BHCs and savings and loan holding companies is the Consolidated Financial Statement for Holding Companies (FR Y-9C).

The number and types of reports that must be filed by a financial institution depend on its size, the scope of its operations, and the types of activities that it conducts either directly or through a subsidiary. The reports filed by larger institutions that engage in a wider range of activities are generally more numerous and more detailed than those filed by smaller entities.

Transactions with Affiliates: An Illustration of Safety-and-Soundness Supervision

Among many topics covered in a safety-and-soundness review of a financial institution, Federal Reserve examiners evaluate transactions between an insured depository institution and its affiliates to ascertain whether or not the transactions are consistent with sections 23A and 23B of the Federal Reserve Act, which restrict such transactions with the goal of limiting risk to the insured depository institution.

<aside>
How the Federal Reserve enforces consumer- and community-oriented laws and regulations

To learn more about the Federal Reserve's enforcement of consumer protection laws and regulations, see section 7, "Promoting Consumer Protection and Community Development," on page 152.
</aside>

Section 23A limits an insured depository institution's loans (and other extensions of credit, asset purchases, guarantees, and certain other transactions) to any single affiliate to 10 percent of the bank's capital and surplus. It also limits such "covered transactions" with all affiliates in the aggregate to 20 percent of the bank's capital and surplus. Securities lending and borrowing transactions—and derivatives transactions that result in credit exposure—also are subject to the limits prescribed by section 23A.

Section 23A also prohibits an insured depository institution from purchasing low-quality assets from an affiliate, and it requires that an institution's transactions with affiliates be conducted in a safe and sound manner. Section 23B requires that most transactions between an insured depository institution and its affiliates be on terms substantially the same—or at least as favorable to the insured depository institution—as those prevailing at the time for comparable transactions with nonaffiliated companies.

Anti-Money-Laundering Compliance: An Illustration of Safety-and-Soundness

Banking organizations are expected to maintain compliance with the Bank Secrecy Act (BSA) and anti-money laundering laws and regulations. Federal Reserve examiners also verify an institution's compliance with economic sanctions imposed by Congress against certain countries, as implemented by the Office of Foreign Assets Control. The Federal Reserve has issued regulations to implement the BSA, including regulations that require banking organizations to establish a compliance program. During examinations of state member banks and U.S. branches and agencies of foreign banks (and inspections of BHCs and certain savings and loan holding companies), the Federal Reserve conducts a BSA and sanctions compliance review as part of its regular safety-and-soundness examination program. The Federal Reserve employs a risk-based supervisory approach to assess a regulated financial institutions' compliance with the BSA and economic sanctions using procedures developed jointly with the member agencies of the FFIEC.

Figure 5.5. U.S. banks operate in more than 60 countries around the world

The Federal Reserve is responsible for examining the international operations of member banks and bank holding companies. As of December 31, 2015, that included operations in the highlighted countries.

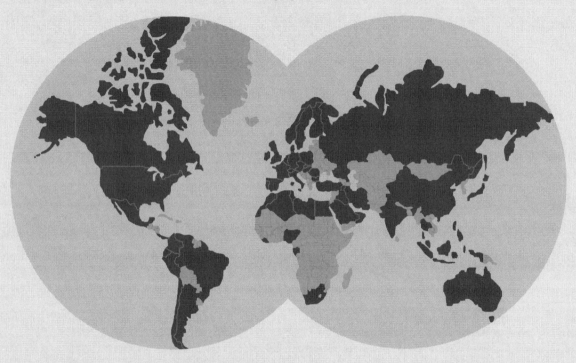

Source: Federal Financial Institutions Examination Council (2015), Statistical Release E.16, "Country Exposure Lending Survey and Country Exposure Information Report" (December 31, 2015), www.ffiec.gov/E16.htm.

Under the BSA, U.S. financial institutions must report large currency transactions and retain certain records, including information about persons and businesses that conduct large currency transactions, purchase certain monetary instruments, and conduct large funds transfers. Furthermore, the BSA requires financial institutions to report suspicious activity related to possible violations of federal law, such as money laundering, terrorist financing, and other financial crimes. Regulations H, K, and Y provide clarification on compliance with suspicious activity reporting requirements with respect to state member banks, Edge and agreement corporations, U.S. offices of foreign banking organizations supervised by the Federal Reserve, and BHCs and their nonbank subsidiaries.

Supervising and Regulating Financial Institutions and Activities

Off-Site Monitoring

In its ongoing off-site supervision of banks and holding companies, the Federal Reserve uses automated systems to (1) proactively identify institutions with poor or deteriorating financial profiles and (2) help detect adverse trends developing in the banking industry.

For example, the Federal Reserve's Supervision and Regulation Statistical Assessment of Bank Risk (SR-SABR) system uses an econometric modeling framework to identify weak and potentially weak banks. By using this system, the Federal Reserve can more effectively direct examiner resources to those institutions needing supervisory attention.

Supervision of U.S. Banks' International Operations

The Federal Reserve has supervisory and regulatory responsibility for the international operations of state member banks and BHCs (see figure 5.5). These responsibilities include

- authorizing the establishment of foreign branches of national banks and state member banks, and regulating the scope of their activities;

- chartering and regulating the activities of Edge Act and agreement corporations (as noted earlier, specialized institutions used for international and foreign business);

- authorizing the foreign investments of member banks, Edge Act and agreement corporations, and BHCs, and regulating the activities of foreign firms acquired by such investors; and

- establishing supervisory policies and practices regarding foreign lending by state member banks.

U.S. banking organizations may conduct a wide range of overseas activities. The Federal Reserve has broad discretionary powers to regulate the foreign activities of member banks and BHCs so that, in financing U.S. trade and investments abroad, these U.S. banking organizations can be fully competitive with institutions of the host country without compromising the safety and soundness of their U.S. operations.

The Federal Reserve examines the international operations of state member banks, Edge Act and agreement corporations, and BHCs principally at the U.S. head offices of these organizations. When appropriate, the Federal Reserve conducts examinations at the foreign operations of a U.S. banking organization in order to review the accuracy of financial and operational information maintained at the head office as well as to test the organization's adherence to safe and sound banking practices and to evaluate its efforts to implement corrective measures. Examinations abroad are conducted in cooperation with the responsible host-country supervisor.

Supervision of Foreign Banks' U.S. Operations

Although foreign banks have been operating in the United States for more than a century, before 1978 the U.S. branches and agencies of these banks were not subject to supervision or regulation by any federal banking agency.

The International Banking Act of 1978 (IBA) created a federal regulatory structure for the activities of foreign banks with U.S. branches and agencies. The IBA also established a policy of "national treatment" for foreign banks operating in the United States to promote competitive equality between them and domestic institutions. This policy generally gives foreign banking organizations operating in the United States the same powers as U.S. banking organizations and subjects them to the same restrictions and obligations that apply to the domestic operations of U.S. banking organizations.

The Foreign Bank Supervision Enhancement Act of 1991 (FBSEA) increased the responsibility and the authority of the Federal Reserve to regularly examine the U.S. operations of foreign banks. Under the FBSEA, U.S. branches and agencies of foreign banks must be examined on-site at least once every 12 months, although this period may be extended to 18 months if the branch or agency meets certain criteria. Supervisory actions resulting from examinations may be taken by the Federal Reserve alone or in conjunction with other agencies. Representative offices of these institutions are also subject to examination by the Federal Reserve.

The Federal Reserve coordinates the supervisory program for the U.S. operations of foreign banking organizations with other federal and state banking agencies. Since a foreign banking organization may have both federally chartered and state-chartered offices in the United States, the Federal Reserve plays a key role in assessing the condition of the organization's entire U.S. operations and the foreign banking organization's ability to support its U.S. operations.

In carrying out their supervisory responsibilities, the Federal Reserve and other U.S. regulators rely on two supervisory tools: Strength of Support Assessment (SOSA) rankings and Risk Management, Operational Controls, Compliance, and Asset Quality (ROCA) ratings. SOSA rankings reflect the Federal Reserve staff's assessment of a foreign bank's

Figure 5.6. Depository institutions and holding companies receive ratings based on the result of examinations and inspections

Ratings, which are assigned to an institution after an examination or inspection, provide a summary measure of the examination's findings.

Rating system	CAMELS	RFI/C(D)
Entity	Depository institutions	Bank holding company Savings and loan holding company

Components	• Capital adequacy
	• Asset quality
	• Management
	• Earnings
	• Liquidity
	• Sensitivity to market risk
		• Risk management
		  – effectiveness of the banking organization's risk management and controls; board and senior management oversight; policies, procedures, and limits; risk monitoring and management information systems; and internal controls
		• Financial condition
		  – an assessment of the banking organization's capital, asset quality, earnings, and liquidity
		• potential Impact of the parent company and nondepository subsidiaries on the affiliated depository institutions
		• the consolidated Composite condition of the institution
		• the **CAMELS** rating of the affiliated Depository institutions

Results	For both rating systems, institutions score on a scale of 1 (best) to 5 (worst) for each factor.	

ability to provide support for its U.S. operations; ROCA ratings provide an assessment of its U.S. branch and agency activities. The Federal Reserve also assesses the entirety of a foreign banking organization's U.S. operations through a single U.S. composite rating.

Under the Bank Holding Company Act and the IBA, the Federal Reserve is also responsible for reviewing and monitoring the U.S. nonbanking activities of foreign banking organizations that have a branch, agency, commercial lending company, or subsidiary bank in the United States.

In 2014, the Federal Reserve Board approved a final rule required by section 165 of the Dodd-Frank Act (which also requires enhanced prudential standards for large U.S. BHCs) to strengthen supervision and regulation of foreign banking organizations. The final rule recognized that the U.S. operations of foreign banking organizations had become increasingly complex, interconnected, and concentrated, and established a number of enhanced prudential standards for foreign banking organizations to help increase the resiliency of their operations. The requirements of the final rule will bolster the capital and liquidity positions of the U.S. operations of foreign banking organizations and promote a level playing field among all banking firms operating in the United States. A foreign banking organization with U.S. nonbranch assets of $50 billion or more is required to establish an intermediate holding company over its U.S. subsidiaries, which will facilitate consistent supervision and regulation of the U.S. operations of the foreign bank. The foreign-owned U.S. intermediate holding company is generally subject to the same risk-based and leverage capital standards applicable to U.S. BHCs. The intermediate holding companies are also subject to the Federal Reserve's rules pertaining to regular capital plans and stress testing.

Finding orders and agreements online

All formal enforcement orders issued by the Federal Reserve and all written agreements executed by Reserve Banks are available to the public in the News & Events section of the Federal Reserve Board's website, www.federalreserve.gov.

Supervisory Colleges

Through participation in supervisory colleges, the Federal Reserve cooperates with foreign banking supervisors, both as the home-country supervisor of U.S. banking organizations with overseas operations and as the host-country supervisor of the U.S. operations of foreign bank-

Box 5.2. A Further Evolution: Taking Corrective Action to Address Troubled Institutions

The Federal Deposit Insurance Corporation Improvement Act of 1991 requires regulators to take prompt corrective action (PCA) to address the problems of troubled depository institutions. The intent of PCA is to minimize the long-term cost to the Deposit Insurance Fund of resolving such institutions.

The PCA framework specifies mandatory actions that regulators must take, as well as discretionary actions they must consider taking, when a bank's capital position declines or is deemed to have declined below certain threshold levels as a result of an unsafe or unsound condition or practice.

The state of a bank's capital position is based on risk-based capital and leverage ratios derived from the bank's Call Report data. Based on its levels of these ratios, a bank can be deemed (1) well-capitalized, (2) adequately capitalized, (3) undercapitalized, (4) significantly undercapitalized, or (5) critically undercapitalized. The law provides for increasingly stringent corrective provisions as a bank is placed in progressively lower capital categories.

Undercapitalized and significantly undercapitalized institutions likely would be required to submit and implement an acceptable plan to restore capital. A critically undercapitalized bank faces receivership unless its condition improves and the activities that expose it to risk are restricted.

More recently, the Dodd-Frank Wall Street Reform and Consumer Protection Act (Dodd-Frank Act) directed the Federal Reserve to promulgate regulations providing for the early remediation of financial weaknesses at bank holding companies with total consolidated assets of $50 billion or more and nonbank financial companies that the Financial Stability Oversight Council has determined should be subject to Board supervision. More specifically, the Dodd-Frank Act requires the Federal Reserve to define measures of these companies' financial condition, including, but not limited to, regulatory capital, liquidity measures, and other indicators that would trigger remedial action. As the financial condition of a company declines, the stringency of the remedial action requirements increases.

ing organizations. This cooperation involves bilateral and multilateral contacts and formal and informal information-sharing arrangements.

With the growth, in recent years, of the international operations of large global financial institutions, the Federal Reserve and other U.S. and foreign banking supervisors have broadened and formalized cooperative arrangements through these "supervisory colleges." Supervisory colleges are multilateral working groups of relevant supervisors that are formed to promote effective, ongoing consolidated supervision of the overall operations of an international banking group. In this regard, the Federal Reserve—in performing the role of a home-country supervisor—organizes supervisory colleges that include the most significant host supervisors of those U.S. banking organizations with the largest global systemic presence. Similarly, it participates as a host-country supervisor in colleges organized by foreign banking supervisors.

Participation in supervisory colleges enhances the Federal Reserve's communication and collaboration with foreign supervisors and supplements bilateral working relationships with foreign supervisors. These relationships are vitally important to the Federal Reserve's supervision of the overseas operations of U.S. banking organizations and the U.S. operations of foreign banking organizations.

Other Elements of Supervision

A Federal Reserve examination can focus on a specific functional area within a regulated entity, such as its fiduciary activities, its securities dealing, or its information technology activities. Furthermore, in light of the importance of information technology to the safety and soundness of banking organizations, the Federal Reserve has the authority to examine the operations of certain independent organizations that provide information technology services to supervised banking organizations, and it examines these service providers on a regular basis.

Results of an Examination or Inspection

Supervisory Ratings

The results of an on-site examination or inspection are reported to the board of directors and management of the bank, BHC, or savings and loan holding company in a confidential report of examination or inspection, which can include a confidential supervisory rating of the condition of the institution. Each state member bank receives a composite rating, which reflects the Federal Reserve's assessment and rating of the bank's capital adequacy, asset quality, management, earnings, liquidity, and sensitivity to market risk (CAMELS). In addition, each BHC receives a composite rating, which reflects the Federal Reserve's assessment and ratings of the company's risk management, financial condition, and potential impact on affiliated depository institutions (RFI/C(D)). Ratings range from "1" to "5," with "1" being the best (see figure 5.6).

The CAMELS supervisory rating for banks and other depository institutions is a tool that all federal and state banking agencies use to convey to financial institutions the agencies' assessment of the institution and to identify institutions whose operations raise concern or require special attention.

Examination Report

In addition to assigning a rating, examiners also prepare a detailed report that, besides formally communicating the rating, (1) describes the institution's activities and management structure, (2) assesses the institution's performance, and (3) recommends changes or improvements in certain policies and procedures.

Enforcement

If the Federal Reserve determines that a supervised institution has problems that affect its safety and soundness, or that the institution is not in compliance with applicable laws and regulations, the Federal Reserve may, by law, take action to ensure that the institution undertakes corrective measures.

Informal supervisory actions. Informal supervisory actions are used to address less-significant deficiencies or problems that the Federal Reserve believes a bank's board of directors or management can correct without the need for more extensive regulatory intervention. For example, the Federal Reserve may address issues detected during the supervisory process by requesting that the institution's board adopt a resolution or enter into a memorandum of understanding to correct potentially unsafe or unsound practices or other deficiencies that do not require elevation to a formal supervisory action.

Formal supervisory actions. If an institution fails to remedy an unsafe or unsound practice or to comply with banking laws, or if the practices or violations are so widespread or serious that recourse to informal supervisory methods is not appropriate or sufficient, the Federal Reserve may take a formal supervisory action, which may compel the institution to take specific actions and which can be enforced in court.

Formal enforcement actions may include

- imposing orders directing the financial institution or its institution-affiliated parties to cease and desist from engaging in the improper or prohibited conduct;

- directing the firm to take certain actions to return to safe and sound banking practices;

- requiring the firm to make restitution or provide reimbursement, indemnification, or guaranty to third parties harmed by the wrongful conduct;

- removing an institution-affiliated party from the banking institution and prohibiting the party from participating in banking at other financial institutions; and

- assessing civil money penalties against either the offending institution or an institution-affiliated party.

Macroprudential Supervision and Monitoring

Ensuring the safe and efficient functioning of the nation's banking system requires that the Federal Reserve consider more than the safety and soundness of individual organizations.

This duty requires that the Federal Reserve also consider factors that can affect the stability of the entire financial system, including the interactions between firms and markets. In other words, the Federal Reserve's supervision includes a macroprudential aspect that focuses on promoting overall financial stability. In this regard, the Dodd-Frank Act explicitly directs the Federal Reserve to routinely factor macroprudential considerations into its supervisory and regulatory activities.

As part of its effort to improve macroprudential supervision, the Federal Reserve Board created the Division of Financial Stability (see section 4, "Promoting Financial System Stability," on page 54). This multidisciplinary division coordinates Federal Reserve efforts to identify and analyze potential risks to financial institutions, the broader financial system, and the economy, and helps develop and evaluate policies to promote financial stability. It also acts as the Board's liaison to the FSOC.

The Federal Reserve also monitors (1) risks that can arise because of substantial interconnections among financial firms and (2) risks that can develop more broadly in the financial system, including at other financial institutions, in financial markets, and in the general market infrastructures.

Financial imbalances can arise, for example, from leverage and maturity mismatch at financial intermediaries, stretched asset valuations, and lax loan-underwriting standards. In addition, the Federal Reserve conducts research to develop measures of systemic risk and to develop a better understanding of how distress at individual firms or sectors can be transmitted to the broader financial system and the economy.

Crisis Management Groups

The Federal Reserve participates in crisis management groups with other state and U.S. regulatory agencies and foreign banking supervisors responsible for the oversight of large cross-border banking groups. The purpose of crisis management groups is to enhance preparedness for, and facilitate the management and resolution of, a financial crisis affecting a large global banking group. Crisis management groups typically include supervisors, central banks, resolution authorities, and other public authorities from jurisdictions with significant operations in the international banking group or respective foreign economy. Similar to supervisory colleges, the Federal Reserve—in performing the role of a home-country supervisor—organizes crisis management groups that include the most significant host supervisors of those U.S. banking organizations with the largest global systemic presence. Similarly, it participates as a host-country supervisor in crisis management groups organized by foreign banking supervisors where U.S. operations of those groups are significant and where the home supervisor has invited the Federal Reserve to participate. This cooperation involves bilateral and multilateral contacts and formal and informal dialogue focused on the development of a framework for early intervention triggers around recovery efforts and resolution planning.

Participation in crisis management groups also furthers the Federal Reserve's communication and collaboration with foreign supervisors and supplements bilateral working relationships with foreign supervisors. These relationships are vitally important to the Federal Reserve's supervision of the overseas operations of U.S. banking organizations and the U.S. operations of foreign banking organizations.

Overseeing the Structure of the Banking System

The Federal Reserve exerts an important influence over the structure of the U.S. banking system by administering several federal statutes that govern the formation, acquisition, and mergers of BHCs, member banks, savings and loan holding companies, and foreign banking organizations.

Under these statutes, the Federal Reserve has authority to approve or deny a variety of proposals that directly or indirectly affect the structure of the U.S. banking system at the local, regional, and national levels; the international operations of domestic banking organizations; or the U.S. banking operations of foreign banks.

Specifically, the Federal Reserve administers several federal statutes that apply to BHCs, financial holding companies, member banks, and foreign banking organizations, including the Bank Holding Company Act (BHC Act), the Bank Merger Act, the Change in Bank Control Act of 1978 (CIBCA), the Federal Reserve Act, and the IBA. As a result of the Dodd-Frank Act, the Federal Reserve also administers section 10 of the Home Owners' Loan Act (HOLA) that applies to savings and loan holding companies, and for administering the CIBCA with respect to savings and loan holding companies.

Bank Holding Company Formations and Acquisitions

Under the BHC Act, a firm that seeks to become a BHC must first obtain approval from the Federal Reserve. The act defines a BHC as any company that directly or indirectly owns, controls, or has the power to vote 25 percent or more of any class of the voting shares of a bank; controls in any manner the election of a majority of the directors or trustees of a bank; or is found to exercise a controlling influence over the management or policies of a bank. A BHC must obtain the approval of the Federal Reserve before acquiring more than 5 percent of the shares of an additional bank or BHC. All BHCs must file certain reports with the Federal Reserve System.

When considering applications to acquire a bank or a BHC, the Federal Reserve is required to take into account the likely effects of the acquisition on competition, financial stability, the convenience and needs of the communities to be served, the financial and managerial resources and future prospects of the companies and banks involved, and the effectiveness of the company's policies to combat money laundering. In the case of an interstate bank acquisition, the Federal Reserve also must consider certain other factors and may not approve the acquisition if the resulting organization would control more than 10 percent of all deposits held by insured depository institutions. When a foreign bank seeks to acquire a U.S. bank, the Federal Reserve also must consider whether the foreign banking organization is subject to comprehensive supervision or regulation on a consolidated basis by its home-country supervisor.

Savings and Loan Holding Company Formations and Acquisitions

Under HOLA, a firm that seeks to become a savings and loan holding company must first obtain approval from the Federal Reserve. HOLA defines a savings and loan holding company as any company that directly or indirectly controls a savings association or that controls any other company that is a savings and loan holding company.

Once formed, a savings and loan holding company must receive Federal Reserve approval before acquiring or establishing additional savings associations. Savings and loan holding companies generally may engage in only those business activities that are specifically enumerated in HOLA or which the Board has previously determined by regulation to be closely related to banking under section 4(c)(8) of the BHC Act. Depending on the circumstances, these activities may or may not require Federal Reserve approval in advance of their commencement.

In general, a company controls a savings association if one or more persons directly or indirectly owns, controls, or has the power to vote more than 25 percent of the voting shares of the savings association, or controls in any manner the election of a majority of the directors of the savings association. A savings and loan holding company must obtain approval of the Board before acquiring more than 5 percent of the voting shares of an additional savings association or savings and loan holding company.

Formation and Activities of Financial Holding Companies

As authorized by the Gramm-Leach-Bliley Act, the Federal Reserve Board's regulations allow a BHC or a foreign banking organization to become a financial holding company and engage in an expanded array of financial activities if the company meets certain capital, managerial, and other criteria. In addition, a savings and loan holding company may elect to be treated as a financial holding company if it meets the same criteria that apply to BHCs and financial holding companies under the BHC Act. Permissible activities for financial holding companies include conducting securities underwriting and dealing, serving as an insurance agent and underwriter, and engaging in merchant banking. Other permissible activities include those that the Federal Reserve Board, after consulting with the Secretary of the Treasury, determines to be financial in nature or incidental to financial activities. Financial holding companies also may engage to a limited extent in a nonfinancial activity if the Board determines that the activity is complementary to one or more of the company's financial activities and would not pose a substantial risk to the safety or soundness of depository institutions or the financial system.

Bank Mergers

Another responsibility of the Federal Reserve is to act on proposed bank mergers when the resulting institution would be a state member bank. The Bank Merger Act of 1960 sets forth the factors to be considered in evaluating merger applications. These factors are similar to those that must be considered in reviewing bank acquisition proposals by BHCs. To ensure that all merger applications are evaluated in a uniform manner, the act requires that the responsible agency request reports from the Department of Justice and from the other approving banking agencies addressing the competitive impact of the transaction.

Federal Reserve Act Proposals

Under the Federal Reserve Act, a member bank may be required to seek Federal Reserve approval before expanding or materially modifying its operations domestically or internationally. State member banks must obtain Federal Reserve approval to establish domestic branches, and all member banks (including national banks) must obtain Federal Reserve approval to establish foreign branches.

State member banks must also obtain Federal Reserve approval to establish financial subsidiaries. These subsidiaries may engage in activities that are financial in nature or incidental to financial activities, including securities-related and insurance agency-related activities.

Changes in Bank Control

The CIBCA authorizes the federal bank regulatory agencies to act on proposals by a single "person" (which includes an individual or an entity), or several persons acting in concert, to acquire control of an insured bank, BHC, or a savings and loan holding company. The Federal Reserve is responsible for approving changes in the control of BHCs, savings and loan holding companies, and state member banks; the FDIC and the OCC are responsible for approving changes in the control of insured state nonmember and national banks, respectively. In

Figure 5.7. Federal Reserve regulations by topic

The Federal Reserve maintains and ensures compliance with the following regulations, which implement federal banking laws and govern the operations of regulated institutions.

Topic	Regulation (by letter and name)		Description
Banks and banking	F	Limitations on Interbank Liabilities	Prescribes standards to limit the risks that the failure of one depository institution would pose to another
	H	Membership of State Banking Institutions in the Federal Reserve System	Defines the requirements for membership of state-chartered banks in the Federal Reserve System; sets limitations on certain investments and requirements for certain types of loans; describes rules pertaining to securities-related activities; establishes the minimum ratios of capital to assets that banks must maintain and procedures for prompt corrective action when banks are not adequately capitalized; prescribes real estate lending and appraisal standards; sets out requirements concerning bank security procedures, suspicious-activity reports, and compliance with the Bank Secrecy Act; and establishes rules governing banks' ownership or control of financial subsidiaries
	I	Issue and Cancellation of Federal Reserve Bank Capital Stock	Sets out stock-subscription requirements for all banks joining the Federal Reserve System
	K	International Banking Operations	Governs the international banking operations of U.S. banking organizations and the operations of foreign banks in the United States
	L	Management Official Interlocks	Generally prohibits a management official from serving two non-affiliated depository institutions, depository institution holding companies, or any combination thereof, in situations where the management interlock would likely have an anticompetitive effect
	O	Loans to Executive Officers, Directors, and Principal Shareholders of Member Banks	Restricts credit that a member bank may extend to its executive officers, directors, and principal shareholders and their related interests
	Q	Capital Adequacy of Bank Holding Companies, Savings and Loan Holding Companies, and State Member Banks	Establishes minimum capital requirements and overall capital adequacy standards for bank holding companies, savings and loan holding companies, and state member banks
	R	Exceptions for Banks from the Definition of Broker in the Securities Exchange Act of 1934	Defines the scope of securities activities that banks may conduct without registering with the Securities Exchange Commission as a securities broker and implements the most important exceptions from the definition of the term broker for banks under section 3(a)(4) of the Securities Exchange Act of 1934
	S	Reimbursement for Providing Financial Records; Recordkeeping Requirements for Certain Financial Records	Establishes rates and conditions for reimbursement to financial institutions for providing customer records to a government authority and prescribes recordkeeping and reporting requirements for insured depository institutions making domestic wire transfers and for insured depository institutions and nonbank financial institutions making international wire transfers

Supervising and Regulating Financial Institutions and Activities

Topic	Regulation (by letter and name)		Description
Banks and banking (continued)	**W**	Transactions Between Member Banks and Their Affiliates	Implements sections 23A and 23B of the Federal Reserve Act, which establish certain restrictions on and requirements for transactions between a member bank and its affiliates
	KK	Swaps Margin and Swaps Push-Out	Implements the prohibition against federal assistance to swap entities
	NN	Retail Foreign Exchange Transactions	Sets standards for banking organizations regulated by the Federal Reserve that engage in certain types of foreign exchange transactions with retail consumers
	VV	Proprietary Trading and Certain Interests in and Relationships with Covered Funds	Establishes prohibitions and restrictions on proprietary trading and investments in or relationships with covered funds by certain banking entities
Federal Reserve Bank activities	**J**	Collection of Checks and Other Items by Federal Reserve Banks and Funds Transfers Through Fedwire	Establishes procedures, duties, and responsibilities among (1) Federal Reserve Banks, (2) the senders and payors of checks and other items, and (3) the senders and recipients of Fedwire funds transfers
	N	Relations with Foreign Banks and Bankers	Governs relationships and transactions between Federal Reserve Banks and foreign banks, bankers, or governments
Holding companies and nonbank financial companies	**Y**	Bank Holding Companies and Change in Bank Control	Regulates the acquisition of control of banks and bank holding companies by companies and individuals, defines and regulates the nonbanking activities in which bank holding companies (including financial holding companies) and foreign banking organizations with U.S. operations may engage, and imposes capital planning requirements on large bank holding companies
	LL	Savings and Loan Holding Companies	Regulates the acquisition of control of savings associations, defines and regulates the activities of savings and loan holding companies, and sets forth procedures under which directors and executive officers may be appointed or employed
	MM	Mutual Holding Companies	Regulates the reorganization of mutual savings associations to mutual holding companies and the creation of subsidiary holding companies of mutual holding companies, defines and regulates the operations of mutual holding companies and their subsidiary holding companies, and sets forth procedures for securing approval for these transactions
	OO	Securities Holding Companies	Outlines the procedures and requirements for securities holding companies to elect to be supervised by the Federal Reserve
	QQ	Resolution Plans	Requires large, systemically significant bank holding companies and nonbank financial companies to submit annual resolution plans
	RR	Credit Risk Retention	Requires sponsors of securitization transactions to retain risk in those transactions
	TT	Supervision and Regulation Assessments of Fees	Establishes an annual assessment of fees on certain bank holding companies, savings and loan holding companies, and nonbank financial companies supervised by the Federal Reserve

Topic	Regulation (by letter and name)		Description
Holding companies and nonbank financial companies (continued)	**WW**	Liquidity Risk Measurement Standards	Establishes a minimum liquidity standard for certain Board-regulated institutions on a consolidated basis
	XX	Concentration Limits	Establishes a financial sector concentration limit that generally prohibits a financial company from merging or consolidating with, or acquiring, another company if the resulting company's liabilities would exceed 10 percent of the aggregated liabilities of all financial companies
	YY	Enhanced Prudential Standards	Implements the enhanced prudential standards mandated by the Dodd-Frank Wall Street Reform and Consumer Protection Act for large bank holding companies
Federal Reserve Credit	**A**	Extensions of Credit by Federal Reserve Banks	Governs borrowing by depository institutions and others at the Federal Reserve discount window
Monetary policy and reserve requirements	**D**	Reserve Requirements of Depository Institutions	Sets uniform requirements for all depository institutions to maintain reserves either with their Federal Reserve Bank or as cash in their vaults
Securities credit transactions	**T**	Credit by Brokers and Dealers	Governs extension of credit by securities brokers and dealers, including all members of national securities exchanges (see also Regulations U and X)
	U	Credit by Banks and Persons Other Than Brokers or Dealers for the Purpose of Purchasing or Carrying Margin Stock	Governs extension of credit by banks or persons other than brokers or dealers to finance the purchase or the carrying of margin securities (see also Regulations T and X)
	X	Borrowers of Securities Credit	Applies the provisions of Regulations T and U to borrowers who are subject to U.S. laws and who obtain credit within or outside the United States for the purpose of purchasing securities

Note: For a list of consumer and community affairs-related regulations, see figure 7.2, "Federal consumer financial protection laws and regulations applicable to banks," on page 158. For a list of regulations governing the U.S. payment system, see figure 6.1, "Federal Reserve regulations governing the payment system," on page 143.

considering a proposal under CIBCA, the Federal Reserve must review several factors, including the financial ability, competence, experience, and integrity of the acquiring person or group of persons; the effect of the transaction on competition; and the adequacy of the information provided by the acquiring party.

Overseas Investments by U.S. Banking Organizations

U.S. banking organizations may engage in a broad range of activities overseas. Many of the activities are conducted indirectly through Edge Act and agreement corporation subsidiaries. Most foreign investments involve only after-the-fact notification to the Federal Reserve, but large and other significant investments require prior approval.

International Banking Act Proposals

The IBA, as amended by the Foreign Bank Supervision Enhancement Act, requires foreign banks to obtain Federal Reserve approval before establishing branches, agencies, commercial lending company subsidiaries, or representative offices in the United States.

An application by a foreign bank to establish such offices or subsidiaries generally may be approved only if the Federal Reserve determines that the foreign bank and any foreign-bank parents engage in banking

Box 5.3. Significant Financial Industry Reform Legislation

Throughout the Federal Reserve's history, Congress has enacted, repealed, and amended significant banking industry laws that have dramatically changed the landscape of the industry. The Federal Reserve has been instrumental in ensuring that these laws are carried out.

For example, during the savings and loan crisis of the 1980s and 1990s, Congress enacted several laws to improve the condition of individual institutions and of the overall banking and thrift industries, including the Competi-tive Equality Banking Act of 1987; the Financial Institutions Reform, Recovery, and Enforcement Act of 1989; and the Federal Deposit Insurance Corporation Improvement Act of 1991. These legislative initiatives restricted banking practices, limited supervisors' discretion in dealing with weak banks, imposed new regulatory requirements—including prompt corrective action (described above)—and strengthened supervisory oversight overall.

A few years later, Congress passed the Riegle-Neal Interstate Banking and Branching Efficiency Act of 1994, which significantly reduced the legal barriers that had restricted the ability of banks and bank holding companies to expand their activities across state lines. In 1999, Congress passed the Gramm-Leach-Bliley Act, which repealed certain Depression-era banking laws and permitted banks to affiliate with securities and insurance firms within financial holding companies.

business outside the United States and are subject to comprehensive supervision or regulation on a consolidated basis by their home-country supervisors. The Federal Reserve may also take into account other factors.

Public Notice of Federal Reserve Decisions

Certain decisions by the Federal Reserve that involve an acquisition by a BHC or savings and loan holding company, a bank merger, a change in bank control, or the establishment of a new U.S. banking presence by a foreign bank are made known to the public by an order or an announcement.

Orders state the Federal Reserve's decision, the essential facts of the application or notice, and the basis for the decision; announcements state only the decision. All orders and announcements are reported publicly in the Board's weekly H.2 statistical release. Information about orders and announcements is available on the Federal Reserve Board's website, www.federalreserve.gov.

How do capital and liquidity differ?

Capital acts as a financial cushion to absorb unexpected losses and generally is the difference between all of a firm's assets and its liabilities. Liquidity is a measure of the ability and ease with which a firm's assets can be converted to cash. To remain viable, a financial institution must have enough liquid assets to meet its near-term obligations, such as withdrawals by depositors and short-term debt obligations that are coming due.

Regulation: Keeping Pace with Innovation and Evolution

Regulation of the financial system must continuously evolve in response to changing laws and conditions in the marketplace in order to ensure that supervised institutions operate in a safe and sound manner.

The Federal Reserve is empowered, therefore, to issue regulations, rules, and policy statements or other forms of supervisory guidance to supervised institutions. Regulations can be restrictive (limiting the scope of an institution's activities), prescriptive (requiring institutions to take certain actions), or permissive (authorizing institutions to engage in certain activities).

Figure 5.8. International evolutions: The Basel Capital Accords

With other federal banking agencies, the Federal Reserve drafts and finalizes rules to implement the capital adequacy standards set by the Basel Committee. Since 1988, there have been three iterations of the Basel Capital Accords; each iteration is phased in over a multiyear period.

Basel I	Basel II	Basel III
1988	2004	2009–11
• Increased capital requirements for internationally active banking organizations. • Reduced international competitive inequities. • Increased comparability of institutions' capital positions. • Introduced measures for market risk for institutions with trading activities of $1 billion or more.	Building on Basel I, Basel II introduced a three-pillar framework for assessing capital adequacy: • **Pillar 1:** Minimum regulatory capital requirements more closely align banking organizations' capital requirements with their underlying risks, including operational risk. • **Pillar 2:** Supervisory oversight requires supervisors to evaluate banking organizations' capital adequacy and to encourage better risk-management techniques. • **Pillar 3:** Market discipline calls for enhanced public disclosure of banking organizations' risk exposures.	Building on Basel II, and in the wake of the 2007–09 financial crisis, Basel III included measures to • improve the quality of regulatory capital to include instruments that are fully able to absorb unexpected losses, with a particular focus on common equity; • increase the minimum quantity of capital that banking organizations are required to hold as a proportion of their risk-weighted assets and provide incentives for banking organizations to conserve capital; and • require global systemically important U.S. and foreign banks to hold additional capital based on measures of their systemic importance.

New regulations may be added, or existing ones revised, in response to new laws enacted by Congress or because of evolving conditions in the financial marketplace. If Congress adopts a legislative change—perhaps in response to a past crisis or problem, or to help adapt the nation's banking laws to respond to changes in the marketplace—the Federal Reserve might issue regulations or rules to ensure that institutions comply with the new law (see figure 5.7 for a list of Federal Reserve regulations and the topics they address).

Evolutions under the Dodd-Frank Act

In 2010, for example, the enactment of the Dodd-Frank Act—the most comprehensive statutory effort to reshape the financial industry since the Great Depression—ushered in many regulatory reforms that help strengthen the financial system and reduce the likelihood of future financial crises. The act calls for consolidated supervision of all nonbank financial companies supervised by the Federal Reserve; requires that

such nonbank financial companies, large BHCs, and foreign banking organizations be subject to enhanced prudential standards; and provides
for the strengthened supervision of systemically important payment,
settlement, and clearing utilities.

The Dodd-Frank Act also required the Federal Reserve and other federal
regulatory authorities to translate the law's provisions into workable
rules, regulations, and guidelines that will achieve the necessary reform
to ensure the financial system's stability and sustainability.

Since 2010, the Federal Reserve, often in cooperation with other regulators, has finalized or proposed dozens of new rules to implement provisions of the Dodd-Frank Act. These rules touched on topics ranging from
residential mortgages and credit scores to risk-based capital requirements
and risk-management standards for certain FMUs designated as systemically important.

Promoting Capital Adequacy and Planning

A key goal of banking regulation is to ensure that banks maintain sufficient capital to absorb unexpected losses.

The Basel Accords: Global Standards for Capital Adequacy

Because of the interconnectedness of the global banking system, the
United States is a participating member in the Basel Committee on
Banking Supervision, the primary global standard-setter for the prudential regulation of banks. The Basel Committee's mandate is to strength-
en the regulation, supervision, and practices of banks worldwide for
the purpose of enhancing global financial stability.

Members of the Basel Committee work together to formulate broad
supervisory standards and guidelines and to recommend best practices
in the expectation that those individual national authorities will take
steps to implement them in their respective jurisdictions, as appropriate
(see figure 5.8). Basel Committee members strive to ensure that banks

Financial disclosures by state member banks

State member banks that issue securities registered under the Securities Exchange Act of 1934 must disclose certain information of interest to investors, including annual and quarterly financial reports and proxy statements. By statute, the Federal Reserve administers these requirements and has adopted financial disclosure regulations for state member banks that are substantially similar to the Securities and Exchange Commission's regulations for other public companies.

are held to consistently high standards and are competing on a level playing field.

Reforms resulting from such cooperative efforts generally aim to address (1) weaknesses or gaps in bank-level regulation, in order to promote resilience of individual banking institutions during periods of stress, (2) systemwide risks that can build up across the banking sector, and (3) the pro-cyclical amplification of these systemwide risks over time.

More recently, the Basel III reforms were designed in part to address weaknesses in the regulatory capital framework for internationally active banking organizations that became apparent during the 2007–09 financial crisis. Basel III includes changes that increase the minimum risk-based capital requirements, introduce a minimum common equity tier 1 capital ratio and a minimum international leverage ratio, and establish a capital conservation buffer designed to limit capital distributions and certain discretionary bonus payments if a banking organization's risk-based capital ratios fall below certain levels.

Capital Requirements under the Dodd-Frank Act

The Dodd-Frank Act requires the Federal Reserve, as well as the other federal banking agencies, to establish minimum leverage and risk-based capital requirements on a consolidated basis for

- insured depository institutions,
- BHCs and savings and loan holding companies that are organized in the United States (including any such company that is owned or controlled by a foreign organization), and
- nonbank financial companies supervised by the Federal Reserve.

The act further requires that the minimum leverage and risk-based capital standards established for these institutions cannot be less than the "generally applicable" capital requirements that apply to insured depository institutions, regardless of their total consolidated assets or foreign financial exposure. Thus, the generally applicable capital requirements serve as a floor for a banking organization's capital ratios.

The minimum capital requirements that are determined using the standardized approach for calculating risk-weighted assets under the agencies' revised regulatory capital framework are the generally applicable capital requirements.

Capital Planning, Stress Testing, and Capital Distributions

Since the 2007–09 financial crisis, the Federal Reserve has worked to ensure that large, complex financial institutions strengthen their capital positions. One aspect of this has been working with firms to bolster their internal processes for assessing capital needs.

Since early 2011, the Federal Reserve has developed and implemented a regular supervisory review of the capital plans of 30 of the largest banking organizations, including in the review any plans the institutions had for increasing dividends or buying back common stock. Through its capital-plan rule, the Federal Reserve requires each U.S. BHC with over $50 billion in total consolidated assets to submit a capital plan annually for review. The Federal Reserve reviews these plans to evaluate institutions' capital adequacy, internal capital adequacy processes, and capital distribution plans. A key objective of this evaluation, officially known as the Comprehensive Capital Analysis and Review, is to ensure firms' capital processes are sufficiently comprehensive and forward-looking.

Part of CCAR is the routine use of stress testing by regulated banking organizations and the Federal Reserve to assess whether an institution will continue to hold sufficient capital to remain a viable financial intermediary even after absorbing the increased losses and reduced earnings associated with stressful economic conditions. If a company is unable to meet its capital requirements under stress tests, or if the company does not have strong processes for managing its capital and evaluating its risks, the Federal Reserve places restrictions on the company's dividends and stock repurchases.

CCAR incorporates aspects of the supervisory and company-run stress tests conducted under the Federal Reserve's Dodd-Frank Act stress test rules. Under the stress test rules, the Federal Reserve conducts annual supervisory stress tests on all BHCs with $50 billion or more in assets, and requires these companies, along with all other Federal Reserve-regulated companies with over $10 billion in assets, to conduct their own internal stress tests. Each year, the Federal Reserve and the companies disclose information about the results of the CCAR and the Dodd-Frank Act stress tests in order to provide valuable information to the public and to promote market discipline.

Liquidity Standards

While adequate capital is essential to the safety and soundness of financial institutions and the financial system as a whole, adequate liquidity is also vitally important. Capital adequacy and liquidity are interdependent, particularly in times of stress.

For example, an institution that is perceived to be undercapitalized may have difficulty borrowing the money it needs to fund itself, while an institution that is illiquid may be in danger of failing regardless of its capital level.

The 2007–09 financial crisis highlighted the importance of adequate liquidity risk management. Many solvent financial institutions experienced significant financial stress during the crisis because they had not managed liquidity in a prudent manner. For example, some institutions had relied excessively on volatile wholesale short-term funding sources and were overly exposed when those funding sources were disrupted.

To address such scenarios, the Federal Reserve and other federal banking agencies issued in 2010 joint guidance on sound practices for managing funding and liquidity risks. This guidance re-emphasizes the importance of sound liquidity-risk management that appropriately identifies, measures, monitors, and controls funding and liquidity risks. The guidance also highlights the importance of cash-flow projections, diversified funding sources, liquidity stress testing, a cushion of liquid assets, and a formal, well-developed contingency funding plan as primary tools for managing liquidity risk.

As a result of the Dodd-Frank Act, the Federal Reserve also established heightened prudential standards for large BHCs, as well as foreign banking organizations with significant U.S. operations it supervises. Regulation YY prescribes heightened liquidity requirements and subjects these institutions to qualitative liquidity risk-management standards generally based on the interagency liquidity risk-management guidance issued in 2010.

These standards would, furthermore, require these institutions to maintain a minimum liquidity buffer based on the institutions' internal 30-day liquidity stress tests. The standards also establish specific related responsibilities for boards of directors and risk committees, require firms to establish specific internal quantitative limits to manage liquidity risk, and impose specific monitoring requirements.

In 2014, the federal banking agencies created a standardized minimum liquidity coverage ratio, or LCR, for large and internationally active firms. Regulation WW requires large and internationally active firms meeting certain criteria to hold high quality, liquid assets that can be converted easily and quickly into cash. The ratio of the firm's liquid assets to its projected net cash outflow is its LCR. To review large firm practices and risk areas not entirely captured in the LCR, the Federal Reserve also conducts its annual Comprehensive Liquidity Analysis and Review, which also serves to evaluate large firms' liquidity positions and risk-management practices.

Margin Requirements: Regulating the Extension of Credit for Securities Purchases

The Securities Exchange Act of 1934 requires the Federal Reserve to regulate the extension of credit used in connection with the purchase of securities.

Through its regulations, the Federal Reserve establishes the minimum amount the buyer must put forward when purchasing a security. This minimum amount is known as the margin requirement. Regulation T limits the amount of credit that may be provided by securities brokers and dealers; meanwhile, Regulation U limits the amount of securities credit extended by banks and other lenders.

These regulations generally apply to credit-financed purchases of securities traded on U.S. securities exchanges and when the credit is collateralized by such securities. In addition, Regulation X prohibits borrowers who are subject to U.S. laws from obtaining such credit overseas on terms more favorable than could be obtained from a domestic lender.

Compliance with the Federal Reserve's margin regulations is enforced by several federal regulatory agencies. The federal agencies that regulate financial institutions check for compliance with the Federal Reserve's Regulation U during examinations. The Federal Reserve checks for Regulation U compliance by securities credit lenders not otherwise regulated by another federal agency. Compliance with Regulation T is verified during examinations of broker-dealers by the securities industry's self-regulatory organizations under the general oversight of the SEC.

Supervision and Regulation Letters and Guidance

Besides issuing regulations, the Federal Reserve also develops public supervision and regulation (or SR) letters, and other policy statements and guidance for examiners and financial institutions.

The Federal Reserve often works closely with other supervisors in crafting these policy statements and guidance. For example, it participates in supervisory and regulatory forums, provides support for the work of the FFIEC, and participates in international forums such as the Basel Committee on Banking Supervision and the Financial Stability Board.

One example of interagency policy development was the 2013 guidance on troubled debt restructurings. This guidance addresses certain issues related to the accounting treatment, and regulatory credit risk grade or classification of commercial and residential real estate loans that have undergone troubled debt restructurings. In addition, the guidance notes that the agencies encourage financial institutions to work constructively with borrowers and view prudent modifications as positive actions that can mitigate an institution's credit risk.

. . . .

Promoting Market Discipline: Public Disclosure and Accounting Policy Requirements

Public disclosure helps market observers and participants assess the strength of individual financial institutions, and the Federal Reserve's role in this regard is a critical element in promoting market discipline. Market discipline, likewise, is an important complement to supervision.

Improved safety and soundness is often realized by heightened market discipline achieved through improved financial reporting and disclosure requirements. Such requirements can serve both institution-specific and macroprudential purposes.

Market discipline can help to restrain imprudent risk-taking by limiting funding of institutions perceived to be relatively risky, and in this way can complement the efforts of supervisors.

Accordingly, the Federal Reserve plays a significant role in promoting sound accounting policies and meaningful public disclosure by financial institutions. Through its supervision and regulation functions, the Federal Reserve seeks to strengthen the accounting, audit, and control standards related to financial institutions.

The Federal Deposit Insurance Corporation Improvement Act of 1991 emphasized the importance of such standards for financial institutions. In addition, the Sarbanes-Oxley Act of 2002 sought to improve the accuracy and reliability of corporate disclosures and to detect and prevent significant weaknesses in internal control over financial reporting (including the detection of fraud). The Federal Reserve has issued guidance to its supervised institutions to address the requirements under these statutory mandates.

The Federal Reserve also is involved in the development of international and domestic accounting and financial disclosure standards. In its mission to improve financial accounting and reporting, the Financial Accounting Standards Board (FASB) has focused on making improvements to simplify the standard-setting process and guidance. Additionally, the FASB and the International Accounting Standards Board continue to work toward converging major accounting standards through joint projects. The Federal Reserve actively participates in the accounting standard-setting process.

Fostering Payment and Settlement System Safety and Efficiency

The Federal Reserve works to promote a safe, efficient, and accessible system for U.S. dollar transactions.

An efficient, effective, and safe U.S. and global payment and settlement system is vital to the U.S. economy, and the Federal Reserve plays an important role in helping maintain that system's integrity.

The U.S. dollar payment and settlement system is composed of payment instruments and methods, systems, and institutions that have changed over time. The Federal Reserve provides currency and operates some elements of this system.

This system facilitates financial transactions and purchases of goods and services and the attendant movement of money at all levels of the U.S. economy—on behalf of individuals and institutions, buyers and sellers, consumers and businesses, investors and securities issuers—and supports interactions between the U.S. economy and others around the world. The importance of the payment system and a sound currency in our daily lives and interactions makes its safe and proper functioning essential to the health of the U.S. financial system and overall economy.

Figure 6.1. The Federal Reserve's role in everyday transactions

Whether you're paying your babysitter, shopping for groceries, or getting your paycheck, you're operating within the payment system. The Federal Reserve plays an important role in maintaining that system's integrity.

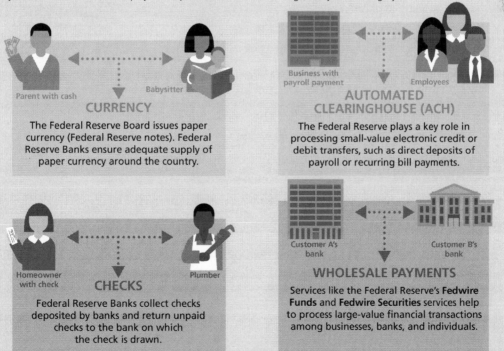

Parent with cash — **Babysitter**

CURRENCY
The Federal Reserve Board issues paper currency (Federal Reserve notes). Federal Reserve Banks ensure adequate supply of paper currency around the country.

Business with payroll payment — **Employees**

AUTOMATED CLEARINGHOUSE (ACH)
The Federal Reserve plays a key role in processing small-value electronic credit or debit transfers, such as direct deposits of payroll or recurring bill payments.

Homeowner with check — **Plumber**

CHECKS
Federal Reserve Banks collect checks deposited by banks and return unpaid checks to the bank on which the check is drawn.

Customer A's bank — **Customer B's bank**

WHOLESALE PAYMENTS
Services like the Federal Reserve's **Fedwire Funds** and **Fedwire Securities** services help to process large-value financial transactions among businesses, banks, and individuals.

Overview of Key Federal Reserve Payment System Functions

The Federal Reserve performs several key functions to maintain the integrity of the payment system. These functions help keep cash, check, and electronic transactions moving reliably through the U.S. economy on behalf of consumers, businesses, and others participating in the economy. They include

- providing services to depository institutions and the U.S. federal government,

- regulating certain aspects of the payment system and supervising certain financial market utilities,

- providing intraday liquidity to payment system participants, and

- analyzing the system to help identify and implement improvements.

All these functions underpin U.S. financial markets and private-sector clearing, payment, and settlement arrangements; support the implementation of monetary policy; and contribute to the overall stability of the U.S. financial system and economy.

The Federal Reserve's Board of Governors in Washington, D.C., and the 12 Federal Reserve Banks located around the nation have distinct but complementary responsibilities with regard to the payment system.

In general, the Board is responsible for developing regulations and supervisory policies for elements of the payment system that fall within the Federal Reserve's jurisdiction. The Reserve Banks help supervise entities under the Federal Reserve's jurisdiction pursuant to these regulations and policies.

The Reserve Banks take the lead in providing accounts and payment services to depository institutions, the federal government, and certain

Major Events in the History of the Federal Reserve's Role in the U.S. Payment System

The Federal Reserve System was created by Congress to eliminate the severe financial crises that had periodically swept the nation by the early 1900s, particularly of the sort that occurred in 1907.

1907

Many banks and clearinghouses refuse to clear checks drawn on certain other banks, leading to the failure of otherwise solvent banks.

1913

Congress creates the Federal Reserve System, giving it the authority to establish a nationwide check-clearing system to eliminate system inefficiencies and inequities.

1918

The Reserve Banks establish Fedwire, the world's first wire transfer system.

1974

The Reserve Banks begin operating their automated clearinghouse service.

other entities (such as government-sponsored enterprises and international organizations), subject to oversight by the Board. The Reserve Banks also provide—subject to Board policies—intraday and overnight credit. Finally, both the Board and the Reserve Banks engage in payment system research and act as catalysts to improve the safety and efficiency of the payment system.

Providing Services to Banks and the Federal Government

The 12 Federal Reserve Banks and their various branches provide a range of payment and settlement services to the banking industry and the federal government. The Banks

- maintain accounts for depository institutions,

- transfer funds electronically,

- collect checks,

- distribute and receive currency and coin, and

- settle payments and eligible securities transactions by debiting and crediting the appropriate accounts at the Reserve Banks.

The Federal Reserve Banks also act as fiscal agents of the U.S. government and certain other entities. In other words, they act as the "government's bank" and maintain the U.S. Treasury's operating cash account; pay Treasury checks and process electronic payments; and issue, transfer, and redeem U.S. government securities.

The Federal Reserve has provided payment services to the banking industry since shortly after the Federal Reserve Banks were established in 1914. At the time, these services were for the most part (1) available only to banks that were members of the Federal Reserve System and (2) provided without explicit charge.

The Monetary Control Act reaffirms the Federal Reserve's role in providing payment services.

2003

The Check Clearing for the 21st Century Act enables the transformation of the check-collection system from a paper-based to a virtually all-electronic system. The Board drafted this law, collaborating with various payment system stakeholders, and the Reserve Banks provided services to accelerate this transformation.

2010

The Dodd-Frank Wall Street Reform and Consumer Protection Act emphasizes the Federal Reserve's role in promoting financial stability and mitigating systemic risk in the financial system and expands its supervision of systemically important financial market utilities and payment, clearing, and settlement activities.

Monetary Control Act of 1980

Congress reaffirmed and expanded the Federal Reserve's role as a service provider with the enactment of the Monetary Control Act of 1980 (MCA), which gave all depository institutions access to the same pricing for the Federal Reserve's payment services and required the Federal Reserve to price specific types of services to recover fully the costs of providing these services over the long run.

The MCA also encourages competition between the Federal Reserve Banks and private-sector providers of payment services by requiring the Reserve Banks to recover not only their actual costs of providing priced services, but also the costs that would be incurred and profits that would be earned if a private firm had provided these services.

The Reserve Banks offer certain payment services in competition with the private sector. The Board has adopted clear policies to avoid conflicts of interest within Reserve Banks that could arise from providing priced payment services and carrying out monetary, supervisory, and lending responsibilities.

Federal Reserve Bank service fees

Under the Monetary Control Act and the Board's Principles for Pricing Federal Reserve Bank Services, the Board is required to set fees for Reserve Bank services to recover the actual and imputed costs of providing these services to the banking industry. The services include check clearing and collection, wire transfer of funds, automated clearinghouse, net settlement, securities services, and new services the Reserve Banks may offer. For the most up-to-date schedule of fees, go to www.frbservices.org/servicefees/index.html.

. . . .

The U.S. Payment System Today and Reserve Bank Services

The U.S. payment system has evolved significantly since the Federal Reserve was established in 1913. At that time, cash and checks were the predominant means of payment. In 2013, 124 billion noncash transactions valued at $1,446 trillion passed through the U.S. payment system. Measured by annual aggregate value, wire transfers, automated clearinghouse (ACH) payments, and checks were the leading payment methods in the United States. Measured by annual aggregate number, however, debit cards, credit cards, and ACH payments were the leading payment methods (figure 6.2). Today's prominence of electronic payments reflects a long-term shift away from the use of checks, particularly in transactions between consumers and businesses.

The Federal Reserve's noncash payment and settlement services are typically categorized as retail or wholesale payment services. The check and ACH services are generally called retail payment services, and the Fedwire Funds and Securities Services and the National Settlement Service (NSS) are generally called wholesale services. These names reflect the lower typical value of the retail services. However, lower-value Fedwire transactions and higher-value check or ACH transactions are also used by individuals and businesses, respectively, to meet their payment needs.

In addition to providing noncash payment services, the Federal Reserve also ensures that the cash (currency and coin) in circulation is sufficient

Figure 6.2. Total noncash payments (Federal Reserve and private sector), 2014

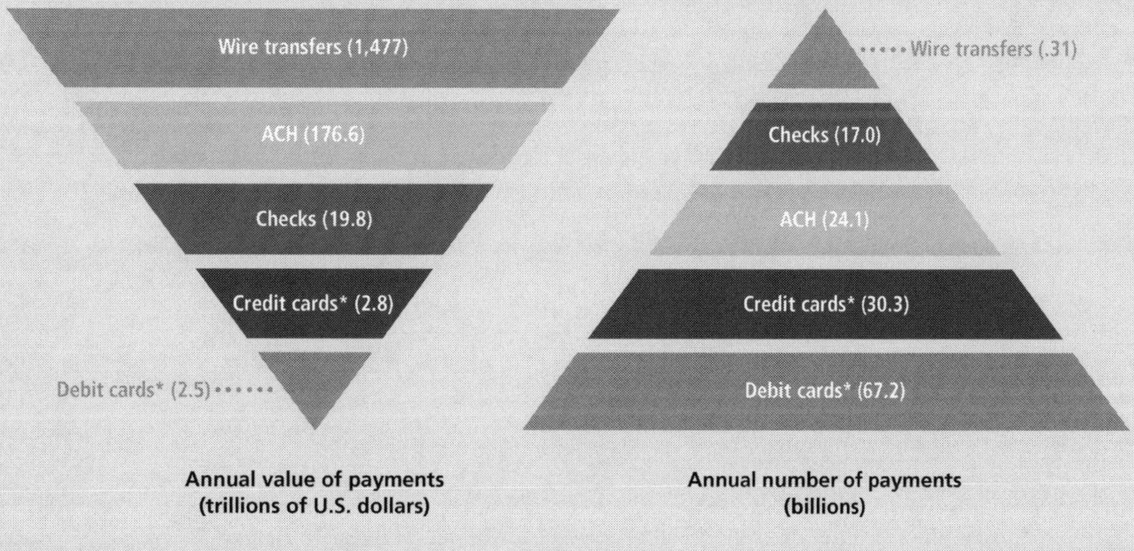

Annual value of payments (trillions of U.S. dollars)

- Wire transfers (1,477)
- ACH (176.6)
- Checks (19.8)
- Credit cards* (2.8)
- Debit cards* (2.5)

Annual number of payments (billions)

- Wire transfers (.31)
- Checks (17.0)
- ACH (24.1)
- Credit cards* (30.3)
- Debit cards* (67.2)

Note: All figures include on-us transactions.

ACH Automated clearinghouse.

Source: Committee on Payments and Market Infrastructures (formerly the Committee on Payment and Settlement Systems) Redbook 2015 except those marked with an asterisk (*), which are projections based on the Redbook 2014. Both are available on the Bank for International Settlements website at www.bis.org/list/cpss/tid_57/index.htm.

to meet the public's demand and that depository institutions have ready access to Reserve Bank cash services.

Retail Payment Services

Guided by public and private cooperation, the U.S. payment system has evolved greatly to better serve all participants in the economy. Innovations and reforms have ushered in greater convenience in many ways, not least of which in the way individuals and institutions conduct transactions between and among themselves.

Check Service and Its Origins

Perhaps no aspect of the payment system illustrates its evolution better than the nation's check-clearing system. The Federal Reserve plays a key role in this system, serving as a major provider of paper and electronic services to depository institutions. In 2014, it collected nearly 6 billion checks, worth more than $6 trillion.

In the early 1900s—before the creation of the Federal Reserve System—the nation's check system was paper-based and used primarily for transactions between banks (interbank transactions) and between businesses. The check-collection system at that time was quite inefficient; for example, banks commonly routed checks circuitously to avoid presentment fees, which banks receiving checks imposed on banks presenting checks for payment. Such routing resulted in extensive delays and inefficiencies in the check-collection system.

When the Federal Reserve Banks were established in 1914, Congress expected them to improve the efficiency of the check-collection system, which would benefit the depositors of checks by speeding up the process and eliminating the practice of paying checks at less than their full face value. This practice of not remitting payment for checks at face value was called "nonpar banking." In 1917, Congress amended the Federal Reserve Act to prohibit banks from charging the Reserve Banks presentment fees and to authorize nonmember banks as well as member banks to collect checks through the Federal Reserve System.

What is the automated clearinghouse (ACH)?

The ACH is a nationwide electronic network, developed jointly by the private sector and the Federal Reserve, for the exchange of electronic files of payment instructions among financial institutions, typically on behalf of customers. ACH transactions are payment instructions to either debit or credit an originator's deposit account at an originating depository institution. The ACH was developed in the early 1970s as a more efficient alternative to paper checks.

What are "clearing" and "settlement"?

Clearing is the transfer and confirmation of information between the payer's financial institution and payee's financial institution. **Settlement** is the actual transfer of funds between the payer's financial institution and the payee's financial institution.

Since then, the Federal Reserve has worked with the private sector to improve the efficiency and cost-effectiveness of the check-collection system. In its early years, the Federal Reserve took a number of steps to reduce nonpar banking. The prevalence of nonpar banking was substantially reduced by the 1920s but did not totally disappear in this country until 1980.

In the 1970s, check volume increased significantly, so the Federal Reserve established additional check-processing offices, called regional check-processing centers, in new locations throughout the country to improve further the efficiency of check clearing. In the 1980s, the Reserve Banks began to offer expanded return check services based on the new expeditious return rules adopted by the Board pursuant to the Expedited Funds Availability Act. In expanding their return check

What is check truncation?

Check truncation is the practice of converting a paper check to electronic information, which is forwarded to the bank on which it was written.

Figure 6.3. What are all those numbers on your checks?

Public- and private-sector coordination and cooperation have led to dramatic improvements in the check-collection process, resulting in more efficient payment and settlement for individuals and institutions.

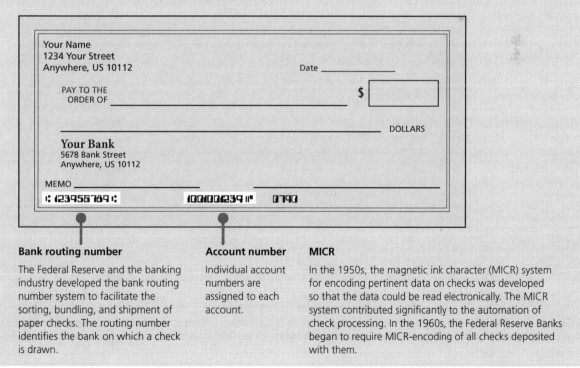

Bank routing number

The Federal Reserve and the banking industry developed the bank routing number system to facilitate the sorting, bundling, and shipment of paper checks. The routing number identifies the bank on which a check is drawn.

Account number

Individual account numbers are assigned to each account.

MICR

In the 1950s, the magnetic ink character (MICR) system for encoding pertinent data on checks was developed so that the data could be read electronically. The MICR system contributed significantly to the automation of check processing. In the 1960s, the Federal Reserve Banks began to require MICR-encoding of all checks deposited with them.

services, the Reserve Banks played a major role in speeding the return of unpaid checks to banks of first deposit—banks in which checks are initially deposited for collection.

Electronic Check Processing

The Federal Reserve served as a catalyst for the transition of the U.S. economy to today's electronic check-processing arrangements (including check truncation). As a general matter, the faster and more resilient electronic check-clearing and check-return methods have markedly improved the efficiency of the nation's payment system while at the same time proving less costly and less error prone.

In the 1990s, the Reserve Banks began offering electronic check presentment services to banks. By the early 2000s, about 20 to 25 percent of the checks the Reserve Banks handled were delivered electronically to paying banks through these services. Overall, most banks continued to simply demand that original checks be presented for payment. As a result, the nation's check-clearing system remained dependent on paper and vulnerable to disruptions in transportation networks.

In 2003, Congress passed the Check Clearing for the 21st Century Act (Check 21 Act), which facilitated electronic check processing by creating a new type of paper document, called a substitute check, which is the legal equivalent of the original check. The Check 21 Act enables banks to remove original paper checks from the check-collection system (called check truncation) and send digital images of checks electronically to banks with which they have agreements to do so, and send substitute checks to banks with which they do not. By creating widespread opportunities for the truncation of checks and associated cost savings, the act has resulted in the nation's interbank check-collection processes becoming almost entirely electronic.

The banking system and the Federal Reserve itself have been able to almost completely eliminate the costly, dedicated air and ground transportation networks that were once used to deliver checks around the country on a daily basis. Further, banks' transition to electronic check processing has enabled them to offer their customers new products and improved service.

Check volume in the United States peaked in the mid-1990s, when about 50 billion checks were written annually. Since that time, check volume has declined significantly as electronic forms of payment, such as debit cards, credit cards, and ACH payments, have become increasingly popular. In response to the growth in electronic check processing and the reduced number of checks being written, the Reserve Banks substantially reduced their costs and physical infrastructure associated with processing checks. The number of Reserve Bank offices processing paper checks declined from 45 in 2003 to just 1 beginning in 2010.

Figure 6.4. Checks collected by the Federal Reserve, selected years, 1920–2014

The number of checks written has been declining as individuals and institutions rely increasingly on electronic means to execute transactions.

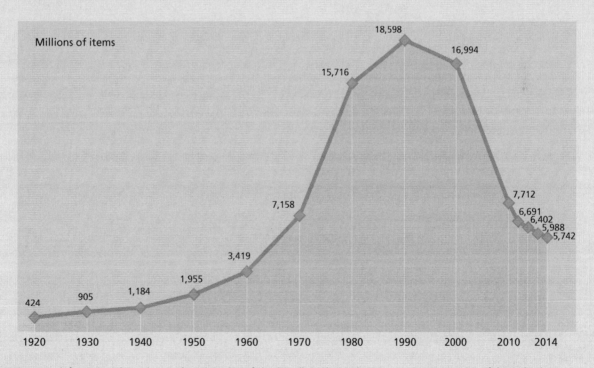

For more information about the number and value of checks collected, visit the Payment Systems section of the Federal Reserve Board's website, www.federalreserve.gov.

Automated Clearinghouse Service

The ACH is a nationwide electronic payment system, developed jointly by the private sector and the Federal Reserve in the early 1970s as a more efficient alternative to checks. At that time, it seemed that the increasing volume of paper checks used by businesses and consumers would eventually exceed the ability of the existing equipment to process and sort the checks efficiently.

How ACH Works

The ACH has grown into a major nationwide electronic payment mechanism that processes files of electronic funds transfers (payments). In general, ACH transactions are either credit or debit transfers. In an ACH credit transfer, an individual, corporation, or other entity (originator) "pushes" or sends funds from its account to that of the receiver. In a debit transfer, the receiver authorizes an originator to "pull" funds from the receiver's account.

The Reserve Banks and the Electronic Payments Network, a private organization, are currently the two national ACH operators. As an ACH operator, the Reserve Banks receive files of payments from originating institutions, edit and sort the payments, deliver the payments to receiving institutions, and settle the payments by crediting and debiting the institutions' accounts. Unlike Fedwire transfers, which are processed and settled immediately, ACH transactions are value-dated—that is, the originator of the ACH transaction includes the settlement date in the payment instructions when they originate the transaction.

In the past, the United States had several regional ACH systems, but over time, the industry consolidated to the current structure of two national ACH systems. In 2014, the Federal Reserve processed more than 11.6 billion commercial ACH payments, worth approximately $19.9 trillion, and more than 1.5 billion government ACH payments, worth approximately $4.9 trillion.

The ACH was originally designed to help automate recurring payments, such as government benefit payments, payroll payments, and consumer mortgage and utility payments. Much of the recent growth in ACH payments has resulted from one-time transactions such as consumer payments initiated over the Internet or telephone.

The Federal Reserve's Role in ACH Development

The Reserve Banks became an ACH operator in large part because of the Reserve Banks' role as fiscal agents of the U.S. Treasury and because of the synergies between the ACH and the Federal Reserve's then-existing check service. The U.S. Treasury, earlier than most businesses, embraced the use of the ACH as a potentially more efficient way to make many of the government's payments, particularly payrolls for military and civilian workers and benefit payments such as Social Security. (Until the mid-1980s, most ACH volume was originated by the federal government.) The combination of commercial and government ACH payments created economies of scale earlier than might otherwise have been the case, allowing the ACH to become a broadly used national service.

Initially, the ACH system relied on magnetic tapes and paper listings to exchange ACH files. Their use required physical transport of tapes between the participants in the ACH system, which made use of the then-existing Reserve Bank national check-transportation infrastructure (e.g., planes and trucks). In the mid-1990s, the Federal Reserve mandated that all institutions' ACH payment files be deposited electronically and all output files be delivered electronically. That is, all institutions dealing with the Federal Reserve directly were required to have an electronic connection to participate in the ACH.

Figure 6.5. Examples of automated clearinghouse transfers
Automated clearinghouse (ACH) transfers can be categorized as either "credit transfers" or "debit transfers" based on the type of instruction sent by the originator of the transfer.

Credit transfer	Debit transfer
• Payroll direct deposits	• Direct debits of recurring consumer bills, such as mortgages, utility payments, and insurance premiums
• Government benefit payments, such as Social Security benefits	• Checks converted by merchants to ACH debits
• Corporate payments to contractors and vendors	• One-time payments authorized over the Internet or telephone

Figure 6.6. Commercial automated clearinghouse transactions processed by the Federal Reserve, 1989–2014

In less than 25 years, the value of commercial automated clearinghouse transactions processed by the Federal Reserve has more than quadrupled.

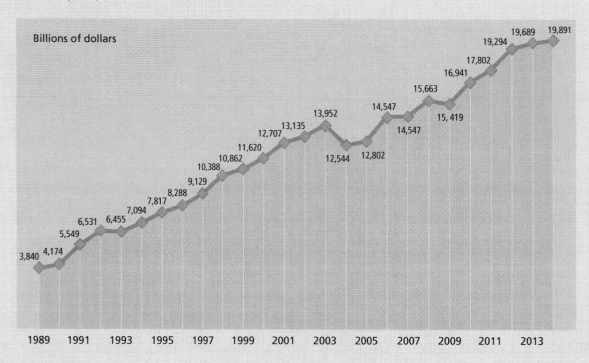

Source: Commercial automated clearinghouse transactions processed by the Federal Reserve—annual data (available in the Payment Systems section of the Federal Reserve Board's website, www.federalreserve.gov).

To provide a more cost-effective mechanism for cross-border payments, the Reserve Banks launched their first commercial international ACH service with Canada in 2001. The Reserve Banks have since established "FedGlobal" international ACH services to Europe and Latin America.

Wholesale Payment Services

Wholesale payments, such as those related to large commercial loans and transactions involving real estate, securities, and money markets, tend to be small in number and large in value, and typically support domestic and international commercial and financial activities. The

Fostering Payment and Settlement System Safety and Efficiency

Reserve Banks operate services designed to support these complex, high-value transactions.

Fedwire Funds Service

The Fedwire Funds Service is a real-time gross settlement (RTGS) system through which participants are able to initiate electronic funds transfers that are processed individually in real time as the funds transfer instructions are received by the Reserve Banks. Once processed, Fedwire Funds transfers are final and irrevocable.

Established in 1918, Fedwire Funds was the world's first RTGS system. It initially used Morse code to communicate payment instructions via telegraph lines. Today, Fedwire Funds relies on secure, sophisticated proprietary data communications and data processing systems to ensure that each transfer is authorized by the sender and not altered while under the control of a Reserve Bank.

Participants—including depository institutions and other eligible financial institutions—use the Fedwire Funds Service to handle large-value, time-critical payments, such as settling interbank purchases and sales of federal funds; purchasing, selling, or financing securities transactions; and disbursing or repaying large loans. Participants also use the Fedwire Funds Service to make smaller-value funds transfers requiring immediate settlement, to make business-to-business remittance payments, and to complete the U.S. dollar leg of international transactions. Fedwire Funds transfers are settled individually by transferring balances held at Reserve Banks from the sending bank's account to the receiving bank's account.

As financial markets have become more global in scope, the operating hours of the Fedwire Funds Service have expanded to increase the amount of overlap with the hours of foreign markets. Fedwire Funds now opens at 9:00 p.m. eastern time (ET) on the night before a business day and closes at 6:30 p.m. ET on the business day. For example, processing on a Monday begins at 9:00 p.m. ET on Sunday and ends at 6:30 p.m. ET on Monday. In 2014, participants used the service to make 135 million transfers worth more than $884 trillion.

Fedwire Securities Service

The Fedwire Securities Service is used by depository institutions and others with a Reserve Bank account to hold, maintain, and transfer securities issued by the U.S. Treasury and other federal agencies, government-sponsored enterprises, and certain international organizations, such as the World Bank. Participants use the Fedwire Securities Service to issue and redeem securities, to transfer securities to settle secondary market trades, to move collateral used to secure obligations, and to facilitate repurchase agreement (repo) transactions. Securities are kept in the form of electronic records held in custody accounts.

Figure 6.7. Electronic payments processed by Fedwire Funds, selected years, 1920–2014

Fedwire Funds is used by depository institutions and other financial institutions to make large-value, time-critical payments.

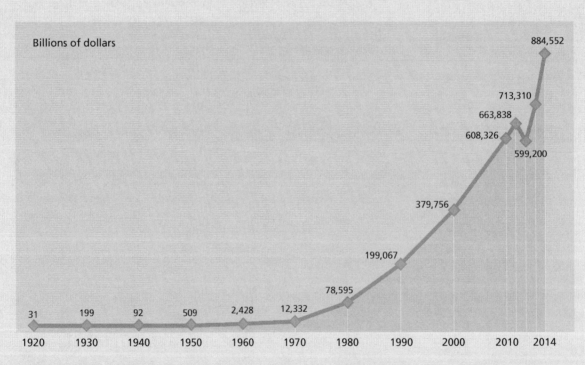

For more information about the number and value of transactions processed through the Federal Reserve's Fedwire Funds Service, visit the Payment Systems section of the Federal Reserve Board's website, www.federalreserve.gov.

Fostering Payment and Settlement System Safety and Efficiency

Until the late 1960s, U.S. government securities were only available in paper form. As securities volumes grew, banks experienced paperwork backlogs and errors. To improve market efficiency and reduce risk, between 1965 and 1967, the Treasury began issuing securities in electronic form and the Federal Reserve implemented computer systems to record, service, and transfer them.

The Fedwire Securities Service operates Monday to Friday from 8:30 a.m. to 3:30 p.m. ET, though participants can reposition securities held in their accounts until 7:00 p.m. ET. In 2014, participants used the service to initiate more than 17 million securities transfers, worth more than $287 trillion.

Figure 6.8. Securities transfers processed by Fedwire Securities Service, selected years, 1970–2014

Financial institutions and other parties use this service to hold, maintain, and transfer securities issued by the U.S. Treasury and other federal agencies, government-sponsored enterprises, and certain international organizations, such as the World Bank.

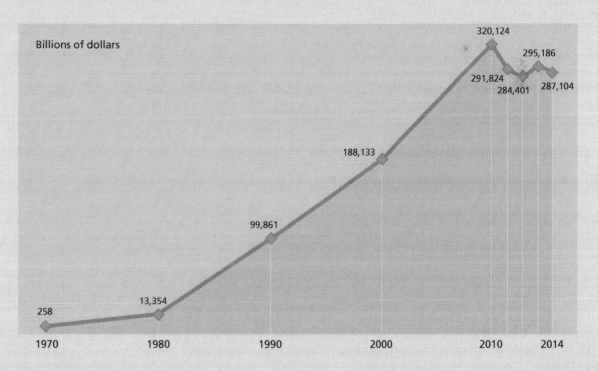

For more information about the number and value of transactions processed through the Federal Reserve's Fedwire Securities Service, visit the Payment Systems section of the Federal Reserve Board's website, www.federalreserve.gov.

National Settlement Service

The Federal Reserve's National Settlement Service (NSS) is used by participants in multilateral clearing arrangements to settle transactions on a multilateral basis through designated master accounts held at the Federal Reserve Banks. Approximately 17 NSS arrangements are currently in use by financial market utilities, check clearinghouse associations, and other entities.

Using an automated mechanism, an agent for a multilateral clearing arrangement submits a settlement file to a Reserve Bank. The settlement file contains a list of the debit or credit positions of the settling depository institutions in the arrangement that are to be settled.

The Reserve Bank first processes each debit individually, crediting those funds to a settlement account on its books. Once the debits have been processed, the Reserve Bank transfers funds from the settlement account to the accounts of the participants with credit positions. NSS reduces settlement risk for clearing arrangements because the funds transferred are final and irrevocable when the debits and credits are posted.

NSS is open Monday through Friday from 7:30 a.m. to 5:30 p.m. ET. In 2014, the Federal Reserve processed about 10,000 net settlement service files, worth more than $17 trillion.

Cash Services

The Federal Reserve Board issues the nation's currency in the form of Federal Reserve notes to the Federal Reserve Banks, which, in turn, distribute currency to the public through approximately 8,500 banks, savings and loans, and credit unions. (The remaining depository institutions obtain cash services from correspondent banks rather than directly from a Reserve Bank.) Federal Reserve notes in circulation are liabilities of the Federal Reserve Banks and are collateralized by the assets of the Reserve Banks.

In contrast, coin in circulation is not a liability of the Federal Reserve Banks. The Treasury's United States Mint is the issuing authority for coin. The Reserve Banks buy coin at face value from the Mint and, in turn, sell it to depository institutions at face value. Coin held by the Reserve Banks is a non-interest-earning asset of the Banks.

Establishing and Maintaining a Reliable U.S. Currency

Although the issuance of paper money in this country dates back to 1690, the U.S. government did not issue paper currency until 1861, when Congress approved the issuance of demand Treasury notes.

Figure 6.9. Design of Federal Reserve notes aims to prevent counterfeiting

The Federal Reserve Board, the Treasury's Bureau of Engraving and Printing, and the U.S. Secret Service primarily redesign U.S. currency to stay ahead of counterfeiting threats and keep counterfeiting levels low.

Security thread.

Hold the note to light to see an embedded thread running vertically to the left of the portrait. The thread is imprinted with the letters *USA* and the numeral *100* in an alternating pattern and is visible from both sides of the note. The thread glows pink when illuminated by ultraviolet light.

3-D security ribbon.

Tilt the note back and forth while focusing on the blue ribbon. You will see the bells change to 100s as they move. When you tilt the note back and forth, the bells and 100s move side to side. If you tilt it side to side, they move up and down. The ribbon is woven into the paper, not printed on it.

Watermark.

Hold the note to light and look for a faint image of Benjamin Franklin in the blank space to the right of the portrait. The image is visible from both sides of the note.

Color-shifting ink.

Tilt the note to see the numeral 100 in the lower right corner of the front of the note shift from copper to green.

For more information on the security and design of Federal Reserve notes, go to https://uscurrency.gov.

All currency issued by the U.S. government since then remains legal tender. Today, virtually all currency in circulation is in the form of Federal Reserve notes, which were first issued in 1914.

As the issuing authority for Federal Reserve notes, the Board has a wide range of responsibilities related to paper money, from ensuring an adequate supply of currency to protecting and maintaining confidence in the currency. To protect the integrity of Federal Reserve notes, the Board works with the Reserve Banks, the Treasury Department, the Treasury's Bureau of Engraving and Printing (BEP), and the United States Secret Service to monitor counterfeiting threats for each denomination and to redesign notes to counter these threats.

New designs of Federal Reserve notes are periodically introduced to make notes more difficult to counterfeit but still easy to authenticate as genuine. The Board manages a program to educate the public on the security and design features in Federal Reserve notes to help protect and maintain confidence in U.S. currency.

The Reserve Banks also help maintain confidence in our nation's currency by ensuring the quality and integrity of Federal Reserve notes in circulation. The Reserve Banks accept and process deposits of currency from depository institutions and credit their accounts at the Federal Reserve. Using high-speed sorting equipment, the Reserve Banks "piece-count" the deposits and remove worn and soiled currency and suspected counterfeits. The fit currency that remains is packaged and returned to the vault, to be used along with new currency to fill future orders from depository institutions. Notes that are unfit for circulation are destroyed. Suspected counterfeit notes are delivered to the United States Secret Service for analysis and final adjudication.

Each year, the Board determines the number of new Federal Reserve notes that are expected to be needed and submits a print order to the BEP. The order reflects the Board's estimate of the additional amount of currency that the public will demand in the upcoming year and destruction rates of unfit currency. The Board pays the BEP the cost of manu-

Figure 6.10. Value of U.S. currency in circulation, selected years, 1940–2014*

The Federal Reserve measures demand for U.S. currency, and the Reserve Banks ensure that depository institutions around the country have ready access to cash.

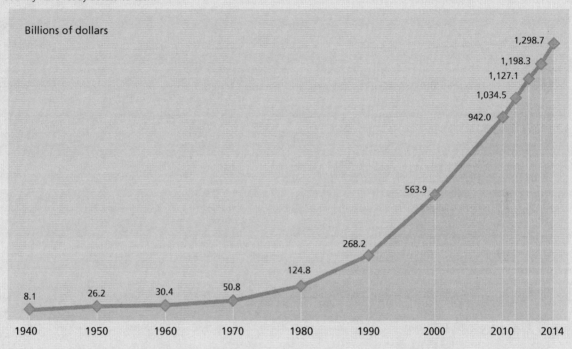

Billions of dollars

1,298.7
1,198.3
1,127.1
1,034.5
942.0
563.9
268.2
124.8
50.8
30.4
26.2
8.1

1940 1950 1960 1970 1980 1990 2000 2010 2014

* Data include Federal Reserve notes and currency no longer issued but exclude coin and denominations larger than the $100 note. For more information about the value and volume of currency in circulation and the volume, value, and cost of the new currency print order, visit the Payment Systems section of the Federal Reserve Board's website, www.federalreserve.gov.

facturing new currency and arranges and pays the cost of transporting the currency from the BEP's facilities to Reserve Bank cash offices.

Demand for currency comes from both domestic and international sources. Domestic demand for currency is largely based on the use of currency for transactions and is influenced primarily by income levels, prices of goods and services, the availability of alternative payment methods, and the opportunity cost of holding currency rather than an interest-bearing asset. In contrast, foreign demand for U.S. currency is influenced primarily by the political and economic uncertainties associated with certain foreign currencies. As of 2014, there were nearly $1.3 trillion worth of Federal Reserve notes in circulation, and the Board estimates that between one-half and two-thirds of the value of U.S. currency is held outside the United States.

Coin

The Reserve Banks' role in coin operations is more limited than their role in currency operations. Although the Reserve Banks store some coin in their own vaults, they also contract with armored carriers that operate coin terminals to store, process, and distribute coin on behalf of the Reserve Banks.

As the issuing authority for coins, the U.S. Mint determines annual coin production. The Reserve Banks order coin from the Mint and pay the Mint the full face value of the coin, rather than the cost to produce it. The Mint transports the coin to the Reserve Banks and the Reserve Banks' coin terminal locations.

Fiscal Agency Services: Acting as the U.S. Government Bank

The Federal Reserve Banks provide a range of services to the U.S. government, acting as the government's fiscal agent. These services include financial, account management, and securities services, as well as application development and technology infrastructure support.

Early History of Fiscal Agency and Depository Services

The provision of fiscal agency and depository services began in 1915 when the Treasury began transferring U.S. government funds on deposit at national banks to its account at Reserve Banks. This action established Reserve Banks as the key intermediaries through which funds are collected and disbursed for the federal government.

In 1917, the Federal Reserve performed the first public debt functions, when Reserve Banks were authorized to receive subscriptions on the First Liberty Loan—bonds issued to help finance the United States' World War I effort. After World War I, the government's need to borrow compelled the Treasury to seek an operational alternative to its limited network of subtreasuries—field offices that functioned as the government's bank in various regions of the country. The Federal Reserve subsumed these public debt-related activities, and the last subtreasury closed in 1921.

Reserve Bank fiscal agency services continued to grow in response to expanding government funding requirements. For example, the financing efforts associated with World War II increased the scope of Reserve Bank fiscal agency functions to include the sale and redemption of Series E savings bonds beginning in 1941. While initially known as Defense Bonds and War Savings Bonds, Series E bond issuance continued until 1980, with millions of Americans purchasing these bonds.

In the 1960s and 1970s, the Reserve Banks' role as fiscal agents expanded to include services—primarily securities-related services—to other federal agencies, government-sponsored enterprises, and international organizations, either at the Treasury's request or through a separate congressional mandate. As noted earlier, the federal government in the 1970s became an early user of ACH services to expedite the processing of government payments, and the ACH now plays a central role in the government's payments and collections.

Reserve Banks currently provide fiscal agency services to a significant number of federal entities. Expenses associated with providing these services account for approximately 15 percent of the Federal Reserve's total operating costs. The Treasury and other agencies reimburse the Reserve Banks for the cost of providing fiscal agency services.

Tax Collections, Payments, and Account Management

The Federal Reserve Banks accept deposits of federal taxes and fees, pay checks drawn on the Treasury's account at the Federal Reserve, and make and receive electronic payments on behalf of the Treasury and government agencies. The Reserve Banks also process U.S. postal money orders and conduct other activities on behalf of certain government agencies.

Collection of taxes was once a paper-based, labor-intensive process, but over time, the Reserve Banks and commercial banks worked with the Treasury to provide secure and convenient ways to process tax collections electronically. In addition, the Reserve Banks operate Pay.gov, a Treasury program that allows the public to use the Internet to authorize and initiate payments to federal agencies.

Disbursements from the Treasury's account at the Federal Reserve are processed primarily through ACH payments or Fedwire Funds transfers or, to a limited extent, by check. The increased use of electronic payments provides the Treasury opportunities to minimize the costs and inefficiencies associated with the delivery of check payments and ultimately to reduce costs to U.S. taxpayers.

The Reserve Banks maintain the Treasury's operating account, provide accounting and reporting services, monitor collateral pledged to the government, and facilitate the investment of excess balances, as directed by the Treasury.

Treasury Security Auctions and Related Services

As fiscal agents, the Reserve Banks auction marketable Treasury securities and reissue and redeem savings bonds. In addition, the Reserve Banks provide securities-related services to federal agencies, government-sponsored enterprises, and certain international organizations under separate statutory authority.

Historically, Reserve Banks employed large staffs to process manually paper-based Treasury bills, notes, bonds, and savings bonds until the advent of marketable book-entry securities in the late 1960s.

Book-entry securities—which are electronic records rather than paper certificates—were created primarily to gain efficiencies in the secondary market for Treasury securities. Beginning in 1986, individual investors could also buy and hold marketable book-entry securities in the Treasury Direct system.

Over the years, the Reserve Banks have adapted their operations in support of the Treasury's securities programs and worked with the Treasury to respond to the declining volumes of paper-based products. The Reserve Banks also work with the banking industry to make use of the electronic check-collection mechanism to collect and process savings bonds submitted for redemption.

Using Technology to Modernize Federal Government Financial Services

In recent years, technological developments—many involving the use of Internet technologies—have provided new opportunities for the Reserve Banks to support the Treasury in modernizing federal government financial services, such as collections and payment processes, governmentwide financial reporting, and debt collection.

The Reserve Banks also actively support the Treasury's efforts to increase electronic payments transactions and reduce paper-based transactions, and to reengineer the government's accounting, reporting, and reconciliation processes. The Reserve Banks have also developed tools to help the Treasury and government agencies verify the accuracy of federal payments before they are made and to assist in the collection of delinquent debt.

Services to Foreign Central Banks and International Organizations

As the central bank of the United States, the Federal Reserve also provides correspondent banking services to foreign central banks and monetary authorities.

The Federal Reserve Bank of New York (FRBNY) provides several types of services to these organizations, including maintaining noninterest-bearing deposit accounts (in U.S. dollars), securities safekeeping accounts, and gold safekeeping. Some foreign official institutions direct a portion of their daily receipts and payments in U.S. dollars through their funds accounts at the Federal Reserve.

If an account contains excess funds, the foreign official institution may request that these funds be invested overnight in repurchase agreements (repos) with the FRBNY. If investments are needed for longer periods, the foreign official institution may provide instructions to the FRBNY to buy securities to be held in safekeeping. Conversely, the foreign institution may provide instructions to sell securities held in safekeeping, with the proceeds deposited in its account.

The FRBNY also provides securities-issuing and paying-agent services to international organizations such as the International Monetary Fund and the World Bank.

Regulating and Supervising the Payment System

For many decades, the Board's authority to regulate the payment system was limited to regulating payments handled by the Reserve Banks. The Board used this authority to regulate check payments collected or returned through the Reserve Banks and to regulate Fedwire Funds transfers.

Beginning in the 1970s, Congress directed the Board to implement several consumer protection statutes governing payments, including the Fair Credit Billing Act of 1974, the Electronic Fund Transfer Act of 1978, and the Expedited Funds Availability Act of 1987 (EFAA). The Dodd-Frank Wall Street Reform and Consumer Protection Act (Dodd-Frank Act) transferred the Board's rulemaking authority with respect to most consumer protection laws to the Consumer Financial Protection Bureau (CFPB), but the Board shares rulemaking authority with the CFPB with respect to the funds availability and disclosure requirements of the EFAA.

During the last two decades, Congress has directed the Board to prescribe regulations implementing a variety of other payments-related statutes. For example, the Board and the Treasury jointly promulgated regulations implementing the Unlawful Internet Gambling Enforcement Act of 2006, which requires designated payment system participants to establish policies and procedures to identify and block, or otherwise prevent or prohibit, unlawful Internet gambling transactions.

In 2010, the Dodd-Frank Act provided the Board additional authority to regulate and supervise certain payment, clearing, and settlement systems and activities that have been designated as systemically important, as well as prescribe rules related to debit card interchange fees. In 2011, the Board adopted rules implementing the Dodd-Frank Act's "Durbin amendment," which limits debit card interchange fees of

Figure 6.11. Federal Reserve regulations governing the payment system

The Federal Reserve has adopted the following set of regulations, which implement certain federal laws governing the U.S. payment system and the operations of participating institutions.

Regulation (by letter and name)		Description
J	Collection of Checks and Other Items by Federal Reserve Banks and Funds Transfers Through Fedwire	Governs the collection and return of checks through the Reserve Banks and Fedwire funds transfers
CC	Availability of Funds and Collection of Checks	Governs the availability of funds deposited in transaction accounts and the collection and return of checks
EE	Netting Eligibility for Financial Institutions	Defines financial institutions to be covered by statutory provisions that validate netting contracts, thereby permitting one institution to pay or receive the net, rather than the gross, amount due, even if the other institution is insolvent
GG	Prohibition on Funding of Unlawful Internet Gambling	Requires U.S. financial firms that participate in designated payment systems to establish and implement policies and procedures reasonably designed to prevent payments connected to unlawful Internet gambling
HH	Designated Financial Market Utilities	Establishes standards and procedures related to the supervision of certain financial market utilities designated as systemically important
II	Debit Card Interchange Fees and Routing	Establishes standards for debit card interchange fees and prohibits payment card network exclusivity arrangements and routing restrictions for debit card transactions

Note: For a list of regulations governing banks and banking, holding companies and nonbank financial companies, and securities credit transactions, see section 5, "Supervising and Regulating Financial Institutions and Activities," on page 72. For a list of consumer and community affairs-related regulations, see section 7, "Promoting Consumer Protection and Community Development," on page 152.

certain issuers and prohibits network exclusivity arrangements and routing restrictions. In 2012, pursuant to the Dodd-Frank Act, the Board adopted rules setting forth risk-management standards for certain financial market utilities (FMUs) and requirements regarding advanced notice to the Board from certain FMUs of material changes to their rules, procedures, or operations.

Expedited Funds Availability Act

The EFAA broadened the Federal Reserve Board's authority to regulate interbank payments, including payments not handled by the Reserve Banks.

The Board initially used this expanded authority to adopt rules to speed the return of unpaid checks. These rules reduced the risk that banks in which checks had first been deposited would have to make the funds from check deposits available for withdrawal (under EFAA's timing requirements) before learning whether the checks had been returned unpaid. In the 1990s, the Board used this authority to adopt its same-day settlement rule, which improved competition between correspondent banks and the Reserve Banks in the collection of checks, spurring further efficiencies.

Electronic Check Processing

To help facilitate the electronic collection and return of checks, in 2001, the Board proposed to Congress what would come to be known as the Check Clearing for the 21st Century Act. The Check 21 Act was enacted by Congress in 2003 and became effective in 2004. The Board adopted regulations implementing the act in 2004. To improve the efficiency of the check-collection process, the Check 21 Act enabled collecting banks to truncate all paper original checks, to send checks electronically to banks with which they have electronic exchange agreements, and to send paper substitute checks to banks with which they do not have such agreements. These changes materially hastened the electronic processing of checks.

Financial Market Utilities

The Federal Reserve regulates and supervises certain financial market utilities. FMUs are multilateral systems that provide the infrastructure for transferring, clearing, and settling payments, securities, and other financial transactions among financial institutions or between financial institutions and the system. These systems include payment systems, securities settlement systems, central securities depositories, and central counterparties.

FMUs play a critical role in the U.S. and global financial system. FMUs often give rise to risks and interdependencies among financial institutions both within and across national borders, creating the potential for widespread financial disruptions if an FMU fails to perform as expected. The Federal Reserve, with its mandate for financial stability, is particularly interested in the smooth functioning of these FMUs and their robust supervision.

The Federal Reserve regulates and supervises certain FMUs under several authorities. The Dodd-Frank Act sets forth an enhanced supervisory framework for FMUs that have been designated as systemically important by the Financial Stability Oversight Council. Among other things, the Dodd-Frank Act authorizes the Board to supervise certain designated FMUs and participate in the examinations of other designated FMUs. The Board also has other authority with respect to certain payment and settlement systems, such as authority to oversee Reserve Bank operations pursuant to the Federal Reserve Act.

The Board may also have an interest in the safety and efficiency of systems outside the United States that provide services to financial institutions supervised by the Board or that conduct activity that involves the U.S. dollar. In these cases, the Board will seek to cooperate with relevant authorities to share information, understand the risks that these systems pose to the U.S. financial system, and promote sound risk management.

Regulation HH sets the Board's risk-management standards for designated FMUs for which the Board is the supervisory agency pursuant to the Dodd-Frank Act. The Federal Reserve Policy on Payment System Risk (PSR policy) (www.federalreserve.gov/paymentsystems/psr_about. htm) sets forth the Board's views and related standards regarding risk management in payment, clearing, settlement, and recording systems more generally, including in payment and settlement systems operated by the Federal Reserve Banks.

Providing Vital Banking System Liquidity

For many years prior to the 2007–09 financial crisis, depository institutions in the aggregate typically held few funds overnight in their accounts at Federal Reserve Banks relative to the trillions of dollars of payments processed daily by the System. To ensure the U.S. payment system's smooth functioning, the 12 Federal Reserve Banks extend intraday credit, or "daylight overdrafts."

Institutions incur daylight overdrafts in their Federal Reserve accounts because of the mismatch in timing between the settlement of payments owed and the settlement of payments due. To address the risk of providing such credit, the PSR policy—adopted by the Federal Reserve Board in 1985 and adjusted since then—controls institutions' use of daylight overdrafts. The PSR policy balances the goals of ensuring smooth functioning of the payment system with the need to manage the direct risk to the Federal Reserve of offering institutions intraday credit.

The PSR policy establishes various measures to control the risks associated with daylight overdrafts. Beginning in 1985, the PSR policy set a maximum limit, or net debit cap, on depository institutions' daylight overdraft positions. Institutions must have regular access to the Federal

Reserve's discount window so that they can borrow overnight from their Reserve Bank to cover any daylight overdrafts that are not eliminated before the end of the day. Beginning in 1994, the Reserve Banks began charging fees to depository institutions for their use of daylight overdrafts as an economic incentive to reduce their overdrafts, thereby reducing direct Federal Reserve credit risk and contributing to economic efficiency. In 2011, the Board revised the PSR policy to recognize explicitly the role of the central bank in providing intraday balances and credit to healthy depository institutions and to provide collateralized intraday credit at a zero fee.

Figure 6.12. Peak and average daylight overdrafts of depository institutions, 1986–2014

The Federal Reserve measures the account balance of each depository institution at the end of each minute during the business day. An institution's peak daylight overdraft for a given day is its largest negative end-of-minute balance.

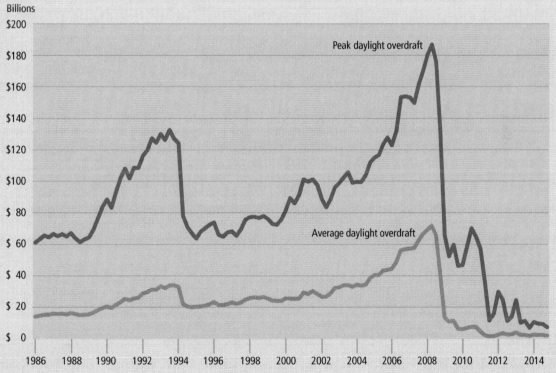

Note: Quarterly averages of daily data. The Federal Reserve measures each depository institution's account balance at the end of each minute during the business day. An institution's peak daylight overdraft for a given day is its largest negative end-of-minute balance. The System peak daylight overdraft for a given day is determined by adding the negative account balances of all depository institutions at the end of each minute and then selecting the largest negative end-of-minute balance. The average daylight overdraft for a given day is the sum of the average per-minute daylight overdrafts for all institutions on that day. Further data regarding peak and average daylight overdrafts can be found in the Payment Systems section of the Federal Reserve Board's website, www.federalreserve.gov.

Managing the Federal Reserve's direct credit risk from institutions' use of Federal Reserve intraday credit can prove crucial because there have been periods during which Reserve Bank exposure to daylight overdrafts has been significant and highly concentrated in a few institutions. For example, after the collapse of Lehman Brothers in September 2008, daylight overdraft activity rose to its highest level since the Federal Reserve began measuring it in the 1980s. Since 2008, higher overnight balances held at the Reserve Banks have been associated with lower levels of daylight overdrafts.

Despite the decline in overall levels of daylight overdrafts, this important tool continues to play a key role in many institutions' efforts to efficiently settle daily payments.

Exploring and Implementing Payment System Improvements

Conducting Research and Analysis

The Federal Reserve conducts research on a wide range of topics related to the design and activities of payment, clearing, and settlement (PCS) systems and financial market infrastructures, as well as the role of these systems in the commercial activities of consumers, businesses, and governments.

Both theoretical and empirical research and analysis of policy issues inform policymakers, the industry, and the public. Research topics include

- design of financial market infrastructure and risk management for complex financial instruments, including derivatives;

- analysis of technological change and market structure in payment and settlement activity;

Figure 6.13. As popularity of electronic payments grows, use of checks declines

The Federal Reserve monitors trends in the payment system, such as the increasing use of electronic forms of payment. Since 2000, the use of debit cards has experienced the most growth, while the use of checks has steadily declined.

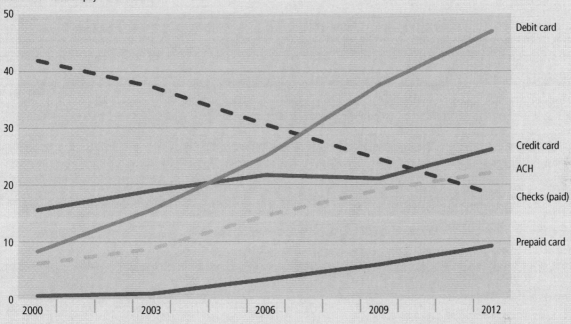

Note: Years in between studies are estimated linearly.

ACH Automated clearinghouse.

Source: The 2013 Federal Reserve Payments Study (available on the Federal Reserve Board's website, www.federalreserve.gov).

- collection and analysis of data on the use of payment instruments and on the drivers of payment behavior; and

- the effect of Federal Reserve policies on market participants, such as the implications of daylight overdraft policy and the effect of payment regulations.

To inform its supervision of financial market infrastructures, the Federal Reserve analyzes financial and technological trends in payments and other financial instruments. Analysis often focuses on economic efficiency and risk, including systemic risk and the impact of financial institutions engaged in PCS activities on financial markets' stability. Some examples of recent research topics include the role of central counterparties in clearing over-the-counter financial transactions and developments and risks in the market for triparty repurchase agreements.

Serving as a Catalyst for System Improvements

As the central bank, the Federal Reserve can act as a catalyst to improve the safety and efficiency of PCS systems, working in cooperation with the private sector and other public-sector institutions, both domestically and internationally.

For example, to help facilitate the electronic collection and return of checks, the Federal Reserve worked collaboratively with representatives of depository institutions, businesses, consumer groups, and the Treasury to develop the draft legislation that became the Check 21 Act. In addition, the Federal Reserve provided leadership, working with other central banks and market regulators to develop and, more recently, to enhance risk-management standards for systemically important financial market infrastructures.

The Federal Reserve has also used its role as a leader and catalyst in facilitating collaboration among industry stakeholders to identify, develop, and implement improvements in the end-to-end speed, safety, and efficiency of U.S. payments. Building on extensive stakeholder outreach and market research, the Board and the Reserve Banks released the "Strategies for Improving the U.S. Payment System" paper in January 2015 (go to www.federalreserve.gov and click on Payment Systems). The paper communicates desired outcomes for the U.S. payment system and outlines the strategies and tactics the Federal Reserve will pursue, in collaboration with stakeholders, to help the country achieve these outcomes. As described in the paper, the Federal Reserve established a task force to identify effective approaches for implementing safe, ubiquitous, and faster payment capabilities, and a task force to advise the Federal Reserve on reducing payment fraud and advancing the safety, security, and resiliency of the payment system.

The Federal Reserve's research efforts may also act as a catalyst for change. For example, the Federal Reserve's payments surveys help inform the strategic plans of payment system participants by providing data and insights regarding payment trends.

Promoting Consumer Protection and Community Development

The Federal Reserve advances supervision, community reinvestment, and research to increase understanding of the impacts of financial services policies and practices on consumers and communities.

7

The Federal Reserve is committed to ensuring that consumer and community perspectives inform Federal Reserve policy, research, and actions, with the mission of promoting a fair and transparent consumer financial services marketplace and effective community development, including for traditionally underserved and economically vulnerable households and neighborhoods.

To fulfill this responsibility, the Federal Reserve performs a number of functions to implement various consumer protection, fair lending, fair housing, and community reinvestment laws and to improve understanding of the dynamics of the consumer financial marketplace, including

Figure 7.1. The Federal Reserve works to ensure that the financial institutions it supervises comply with laws that protect consumers

Federal Reserve survey data show that nearly all American families are involved in the financial services marketplace, whether as bank account holders, credit card users, or borrowers. The Federal Reserve's consumer-focused supervision and regulation, research and analysis, and community engagement programs help ensure that consumer and community perspectives inform supervisory and policy work.

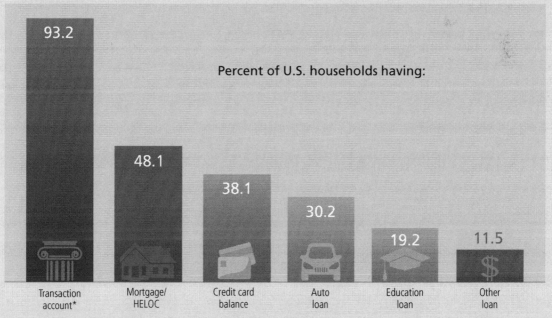

Percent of U.S. households having:

Transaction account*	Mortgage/HELOC	Credit card balance	Auto loan	Education loan	Other loan
93.2	48.1	38.1	30.2	19.2	11.5

* Transaction account includes checking, savings, and money market deposit accounts; money market mutual funds; and call or cash accounts at brokerages.

HELOC Home equity line of credit.

Source: 2013 Survey of Consumer Finances (available in the Economic Research & Data section of the Federal Reserve Board's website, www.federalreserve.gov).

- formulating and carrying out consumer-focused supervision and examination policy to ensure that financial institutions under its jurisdiction comply with applicable consumer protection laws and regulations and meet the requirements of community reinvestment laws and regulations;

- conducting rigorous research, analysis, and data collection to identify emerging consumer financial issues and assess their implications for economic and supervisory policy;

- engaging, convening, and informing key stakeholders to identify emerging issues and policies and practices to advance effective community reinvestment and consumer protection; and

- writing and reviewing regulations that implement consumer protection and community reinvestment laws.

· ·

Consumer-Focused Supervision and Examination

Various consumer protection, fair lending, fair housing, and community reinvestment laws apply to how financial institutions interact with their customers and their communities. A primary Federal Reserve responsibility to consumers is to ensure that the financial institutions under its jurisdiction comply with applicable laws and regulations established by Congress and the federal regulatory agencies.

Who the Federal Reserve Supervises for Consumer Protection Laws and Regulations

The Federal Reserve supervises state member banks for compliance with consumer- and community-oriented laws (for a full discussion of state member banks, see section 5, "Supervising and Regulating Financial Institutions and Activities," on page 72). The Federal Reserve evaluates

- performance under the Community Reinvestment Act (CRA) for all state member banks, regardless of size;

- compliance by all state member banks, regardless of size, and their affiliates with the Fair Housing Act, the Servicemembers Civil Relief Act, the National Flood Insurance Act, prohibitions on unfair or deceptive acts or practices (UDAP) under the Federal Trade Commission Act, and certain other federal consumer financial protection laws not specifically under the Consumer Financial Protection Bureau's authority; and

- compliance by state member banks with total assets of $10 billion or less with all federal consumer financial protection laws and regulations. (See figure 7.2.)

In addition, the Federal Reserve serves as the consolidated supervisor for all bank holding companies and ensures that consumer compliance risk is appropriately incorporated into a holding company's consolidated supervision rating. The Federal Reserve has additional supervisory responsibility as the federal supervisor for savings and loan holding companies and the consolidated supervisor for foreign banking organizations and nonbank financial companies designated by the Financial Stability Oversight Council for supervision by the Federal Reserve under the Dodd-Frank Wall Street Reform and Consumer Protection Act. (For more details on entities the Federal Reserve supervises, see section 5, "Supervising and Regulating Financial Institutions and Activities," on page 72.)

How the Federal Reserve Supervises for Consumer Protection Laws and Regulations

The Federal Reserve Board of Governors, and the 12 Reserve Banks under delegated authority, have responsibilities for consumer compliance supervision of organizations under the Federal Reserve's jurisdiction.

The Board develops consumer compliance supervisory policies and identifies emerging issues; provides rigorous examiner training; and assists with the enforcement of fair lending, UDAP, and flood insurance violations. Further, the Board evaluates applications involving bank or thrift holding companies or state member banks that present CRA or consumer compliance issues, or that receive adverse comments from external parties. The Board also works with other agencies to promote consistency in examination principles, standards, and processes. The Board's Division of Consumer and Community Affairs (DCCA) provides support to the Board in its consumer-focused supervisory activities.

A Regional Approach to Supervision

The Federal Reserve employs a regionalized approach to supervision. The Board has delegated its examination authority to the 12 Reserve Banks, which maintain consumer compliance supervisory programs that evaluate institutions for their level of compliance with applicable consumer protection laws, using policies set by the Board. Each Reserve Bank has a staff of examiners who conduct periodic compliance examinations at financial institutions under the Federal Reserve's supervisory authority, including state member banks and bank holding companies. Consumer compliance examiners review the policies and practices that pertain to consumer products and services offered at each of these institutions. The Board oversees these Reserve Bank programs and routinely evaluates their effectiveness.

The network of Reserve Banks across the United States is integral to the implementation of the Federal Reserve's supervisory policy and helps inform the Board's understanding of consumer financial services trends and issues that may be specific to some regions of the country.

Insights and examination findings from the Reserve Banks support the Federal Reserve's efforts to ensure that banking institutions effectively serve consumers and communities and treat consumers fairly in their credit and financial transactions.

Risk-Focused Consumer Compliance Supervision

The Federal Reserve applies a risk-focused approach to consumer compliance supervision, focusing most intensely on those areas involving the greatest compliance risk. This approach is designed to promote strong compliance risk management practices at financial institutions and to enhance the efficacy of the Federal Reserve's supervision program while managing regulatory burden on many community banking organizations.

Under the Federal Reserve's risk-focused consumer compliance program for community banks, consumer compliance examiners follow procedures for assessing an individual financial institution's risk profile, including its consumer compliance culture and how effectively it identifies and manages consumer compliance risk, to determine the scope and resources needed when conducting an examination. The risk-focused examination program also incorporates ongoing supervision to help identify and, if necessary, address significant changes in the institution's compliance risk management program or in the level of consumer compliance risk present, as well as to ensure that supervisory information is up to date.

The Federal Reserve also maintains a risk-focused program for assessing consumer compliance risk at bank holding companies in the System, to ensure that consumer compliance risk is effectively integrated into the holding company rating.

Supervisory Policies and Guidance

The Federal Reserve communicates significant consumer-related policy and procedural matters through Consumer Affairs (CA) supervisory letters. The Federal Reserve often works closely with other supervisors in crafting policy statements and guidance. CA letters can address a wide range of topics, such as foreclosures, privacy of consumer financial information, special legal protections for service members' credit transactions, and examination procedures for various consumer protection laws and regulations and the CRA.

Interagency Initiatives

Through its participation on the Federal Financial Institutions Examination Council (FFIEC), the Federal Reserve collaborates with other federal and state banking agencies on consumer financial supervisory guid-

Consumer Affairs (CA) letters

To see the wide range of consumer issues addressed by the Federal Reserve through CA letters, visit the Banking Information & Regulation section, subsection Supervision, of the Board's website at www.federalreserve.gov/bankinforeg/caletters/caletters.htm.

Figure 7.2. Federal consumer financial protection laws and regulations applicable to banks

Financial institutions must comply with a variety of laws and regulations that protect consumers. The Federal Reserve Banks, using policies set by the Board of Governors, maintain consumer compliance supervisory programs that evaluate institutions for their level of compliance with applicable consumer protection laws.

General banking	
Federal Trade Commission Act	Prohibits unfair or deceptive acts or practices in any aspect of banking transactions.
Gramm-Leach-Bliley Act (title V, subpart A), Disclosure of Nonpublic Personal Information*	Describes the conditions under which a financial institution may disclose nonpublic personal information about consumers to nonaffiliated third parties, provides a method for consumers to opt out of information sharing with nonaffiliated third parties, and requires a financial institution to notify consumers about its privacy policies and practices.

Depository accounts	
Electronic Fund Transfer Act/ Regulation E*	Requires disclosure of the terms and conditions of electronic fund transfers. Protects consumers against unauthorized transfers and establishes procedures for resolving errors and disputes.
Expedited Funds Availability Act/ Regulation CC	Limits hold periods on deposits made to depository institutions and requires appropriate consumer disclosures.
Truth in Savings Act /Regulation DD*	Requires uniform disclosure of terms and conditions regarding interest rates and fees associated with deposit accounts. Prohibits misleading and inaccurate advertisements.

Credit/general lending	
Truth in Lending Act/Regulation Z*	Requires lenders to clearly disclose lending terms and costs to borrowers, and incorporates the provisions of the Credit Card Accountability Responsibility and Disclosure Act, Fair Credit Billing Act, Fair Credit and Charge Card Disclosure Act, Home Equity Loan Consumer Protection Act, and Home Ownership and Equity Protection Act.
Fair Credit Reporting Act*	Protects consumers from unfair credit reporting practices and requires credit-reporting agencies to allow credit applicants to correct inaccurate credit reports.
Equal Credit Opportunity Act/ Regulation B*	Prohibits creditors from discriminating on the basis of race, color, national origin, religion, sex, marital status, age, receipt of public assistance, and exercise of rights under the Consumer Credit Protection Act.
Community Reinvestment Act/ Regulation BB	Encourages financial institutions to help meet the credit needs of their entire communities, including low- and moderate-income neighborhoods.

Promoting Consumer Protection and Community Development

Disclosure and Reporting of CRA-Related Agreements/Regulation G	Requires banks and their affiliates and other parties to make public certain agreements that are in fulfillment of the Community Reinvestment Act, and to file annual reports concerning the agreements with the appropriate agency.
Fair and Accurate Credit Transaction Act*	Amends the Fair Credit Reporting Act. Enhances consumers' ability to combat identity theft, increases the accuracy of consumer reports, allows consumers to exercise greater control over the type and amount of marketing solicitations they receive, restricts the use and disclosure of sensitive medical information, and establishes uniform national standards in the regulation of consumer reporting.
Servicemembers Civil Relief Act and Military Lending Act	Provides members of the military certain financial protections while on active duty.

Mortgage lending

Fair Housing Act	Prohibits discrimination in the sale, rental, and financing of dwellings and housing-related transactions on the basis of race, color, national origin, religion, sex, handicap, or familial status.
Real Estate Settlement Procedures Act/Regulation X*	Requires that the nature and costs of real estate settlements be disclosed to borrowers. Also protects borrowers against abusive practices, such as kickbacks, and regulates the use of escrow accounts.
Home Mortgage Disclosure Act/Regulation C*	Requires mortgage lenders to annually disclose to the public data on the geographic distribution of applications and loans for originations, purchases, home-improvement, and refinancings. Requires lenders to report data on the ethnicity, race, sex, income of applicants and borrowers, and other data. Also directs the Federal Financial Institutions Examination Council, of which the Federal Reserve is a member, to make summaries of the data available to the public.

Other financial topics

Flood Disaster Protection Act/Regulation H	Requires flood insurance in connection with loans secured by property located in a flood hazard area designated under the National Flood Insurance Program.
Consumer Leasing Act/Regulation M*	Requires disclosure of information about the costs and terms of consumer leases for vehicles and other personal property.

* The Federal Reserve System does not examine for these laws and regulations for depository institutions with total assets in excess of $10 billion.

ance. The FFIEC works to develop uniform principles, standards, and report forms for the federal examinations of financial institutions. These efforts promote the goal of supervisory consistency and uniformity across the banking industry.

The Board's FFIEC representative is advised by DCCA staff regarding policy, procedures, and guidance related to consumer compliance supervision. For more information on interagency supervisory initiatives, see "Oversight Councils" on page 81.

How the Federal Reserve Enforces Consumer Protection Laws and Rules

After a consumer compliance examination, examiners issue a confidential report of examination, which includes a consumer compliance program rating that reflects the institution's performance with regard to consumer compliance. When an examination reveals that an institution's policies or practices do not comply with consumer protection rules and regulations, examiners cite violations in the report of examination and require management to correct the violations and address any program deficiencies. The Federal Reserve also has additional supervisory tools to ensure that bank management addresses consumer compliance program weaknesses, including informal and formal enforcement actions.

Formal enforcement actions include

- executing a written agreement between the Federal Reserve and the financial institution's board of directors or its management that requires the institution to take specified corrective action;

- issuing cease-and-desist orders to halt practices in violation;

- assessing civil money penalties, when appropriate, depending on the nature, severity, and degree of harm to consumers as a result of deficient practices; and

- ordering remedies or restitution to consumers affected by an institution's violations.

Box 7.1. Making Compliance with Consumer Laws a Priority

The Federal Reserve's consumer compliance supervision program is founded on the expectation that consumer compliance risk management is an integral part of an institution's corporate-wide risk management.

A key goal is ensuring that each institution is in full compliance with federal consumer protection laws and regulations and has processes and programs in place to keep up with new or revised compliance requirements that may arise as laws, regulations, and bank products and services change. Examiners look for a number of indicators of an institution's management of consumer compliance risk:

- **Board of directors and senior management oversight.** Directors have ultimate responsibility for the risk taken by their institutions. Examiners seek to ensure that senior management is implementing strategies that effectively identify and control for consumer compliance risk.

- **Policies and procedures.** Examiners seek to ensure that an effective compliance program is in place with documented policies, procedures, and processes for monitoring and controlling compliance risks.

- **Risk monitoring.** Examiners seek to ensure that information management systems provide timely reports

to management on an institution's financial condition, operating performance, and risk exposure.

- **Internal controls.** Examiners seek to ensure that an institution's internal control structure allows it to effectively manage its consumer compliance risk, and creates effective lines of authority and responsibility.

- **Training.** Examiners seek to ensure that an institution provides its personnel with training regarding rules, regulations, policies, and procedures that impact the institution's business lines.

Evaluating Performance under the Community Reinvestment Act

The Community Reinvestment Act encouraged depository institutions—commercial banks and savings institutions—to help meet the credit needs of their local communities, including low- and moderate-income neighborhoods, consistent with safe and sound operations. The CRA requires the Federal Reserve to evaluate each state member bank's CRA performance and assign one of four CRA ratings—Outstanding, Satisfactory, Needs to Improve, or Substantial Noncompliance. The CRA rating and conclusions, as well as the facts, data, and analysis that support the bank's rating, are summarized in a publicly available performance evaluation.

CRA examiners assess a bank's performance using examination procedures tailored to the bank's size and the type of business it does. Performance is evaluated in the context of the institution and the communities within which it operates. That means examiners consider information about the bank's business strategy, product offerings, capacity, and constraints, as well as the economic conditions, lending, investment, and service needs and opportunities in the bank's communities.

The public can also play a role in the CRA examination process by offering comments on an institution's CRA performance, which the financial institution must make accessible to the public. Examiners review these comments and consider them when evaluating a bank's overall CRA performance.

An institution's CRA rating and comments from the public are also considered when the institution applies to open additional branches or to engage in a merger or acquisition. The public has the opportunity to submit written comments on an application. These comments are considered by the Board when it evaluates the application.

Responding to Consumer Feedback

In addition to on-site examiner reviews of financial institutions, Federal Reserve staff identify and investigate possible violations of consumer protection laws through the Federal Reserve System's consumer complaint and consumer inquiry programs. Through these programs, staff answer consumers' questions, explain consumer rights under federal law, investigate complaints against entities supervised by the Federal Reserve, and refer complaints about other entities to the appropriate agency. Consumer complaints are a critical component of the risk-focused supervisory program. The Federal Reserve uses data on consumer complaint activity in its supervisory processes when monitoring financial institutions, scoping and conducting examinations, and analyzing applications. Information about consumer complaints is also reported in the Federal Reserve Board's Annual Report to Congress (available at www.federalreserve.gov).

Handling Complaints

The Federal Reserve has uniform policies and procedures for investigating and responding to consumer complaints, which are implemented by staff at the 12 Federal Reserve Banks and the Federal Reserve Con-

Public comments on CRA performance

Public feedback about a depository institution's record in meeting the credit needs of its community helps inform the Federal Reserve's overall evaluation of that institution's compliance with the Community Reinvestment Act (CRA) and its decisions about a bank's application to open more branches or complete a merger or acquisition. For information on submitting comments about a bank's CRA performance, see www.federalreserve.gov/communitydev/cra_about.htm. For information on submitting comments on banking applications, visit www.federalreserve.gov/bankinforeg/afi/cra.htm.

sumer Help (FRCH) Center. The FRCH is a centralized consumer complaint and inquiry processing center, which allows consumers to contact the Federal Reserve online or by telephone, fax, mail, or e-mail.

When a consumer files a complaint with the FRCH, the first step is to determine which Reserve Bank or other banking agency has responsibility for investigating that complaint. If the complaint involves an entity that is not supervised by the Federal Reserve, the FRCH forwards the complaint to the appropriate agency and then tells the consumer how to contact that agency. If a complaint involves an institution supervised by the Federal Reserve System, the FRCH forwards it to the Reserve Bank that examines the institution in question to conduct an investigation. The FRCH typically responds to consumers within 15 business days of the complaint submission.

After receiving the complaint from the FRCH, the Reserve Bank forwards the consumer complaint to the institution to obtain a written response. During the complaint investigation, the Reserve Bank analyzes the documentation provided by the consumer and the institution to determine if the institution violated a law, handled the situation correctly, or corrected an error. The Reserve Bank communicates the outcome of the investigation to the consumer in writing.

Addressing Inquiries and Potential Financial Scams

The FRCH receives thousands of consumer inquiries on a wide range of topics each year. FRCH staff strive to provide consumers with information about their rights to enable an understanding of financial products and services, which may be useful in future financial decisionmaking. The FRCH website offers information about many of these topics—credit cards, checking accounts, electronic banking, mortgages, and foreclosures. Consumers are directed to resources offered by federal agencies and trusted organizations to get accurate and straightforward information to answer their questions.

The FRCH also empowers consumers to recognize and report potential scams. The FRCH website contains information alerting consumers to

Box 7.2. Federal Reserve Consumer Help: Responding to Consumer Complaints and Inquiries

Federal Reserve Consumer Help (FRCH), a centralized consumer complaint and inquiry processing center, allows consumers to contact the Federal Reserve online or by telephone, fax, mail, or e-mail.

The FRCH website (www.federalreserve consumerhelp.gov) is a resource for consumers to learn about financial products and services and provides instructions on how to file a consumer complaint with the Federal Reserve.

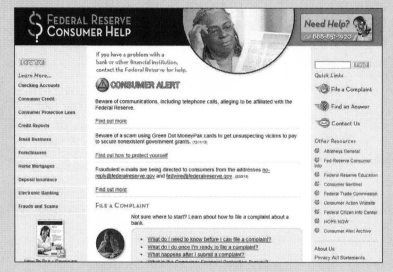

characteristics of a scam and provides a link for reporting the information on a product or service they suspect is a scam.

Administering Consumer Laws, Drafting Regulations

The Federal Reserve Board has rulemaking responsibility under specific statutory provisions of the consumer financial services and fair lending laws. The Board issues regulations to implement those laws and also issues (directly or through staff) official interpretations and compliance guidance for the financial industry and for the Reserve Banks' examination staff.

The Board also regularly works with other federal financial regulatory agencies in proposing rules and procedures to implement new laws and amendments to existing laws. For example, the Board collaborates with the Consumer Financial Protection Bureau, the Federal Deposit Insurance Corporation, the National Credit Union Administration, the Office of the Comptroller of the Currency, and the Federal Housing Finance Agency to establish appraisal requirements for home mortgage transactions. Joint efforts such as these aim to ensure that consumer protections mandated by the Congress are enforced effectively across all institutions.

Research and Analysis of Emerging Consumer Issues

Thorough research and analysis about consumers, their financial experiences, and the communities in which they live inform Federal Reserve policymaking.

Thus, the Board and the Reserve Banks collaborate to identify trends and emerging issues that impact the financial livelihood and well-being of consumers and communities. This effort relies on a variety of resources, including a wealth of data collected through surveys and independent research. Findings from compliance examinations and trends in consumer complaints also help to shed light on emerging issues. Sources of data and information continually evolve as information resources and technology provide better insights into the financial services and community development issues of consumers and neighborhoods.

To inform its research efforts, the Federal Reserve conducts consumer focus groups, outreach to consumer and community groups, outreach to academic and policy organizations, and consumer surveys to gain insight into trends in consumer financial services, community economic development, and policy matters. This information and data contributes to the Federal Reserve's work and provides the consumer perspective for other Federal Reserve System functions.

Figure 7.3. Federal Reserve research examines trends and issues in consumer financial services

The Federal Reserve Board conducts the annual Survey of Household Economics and Decisionmaking (SHED), a nationally representative survey that evaluates the economic well-being of U.S. households and identifies potential risks to their financial stability. The survey includes modules on a range of topics of current relevance to financial well-being, including housing, credit access and behaviors, savings, retirement, economic fragility, and education and student loans.

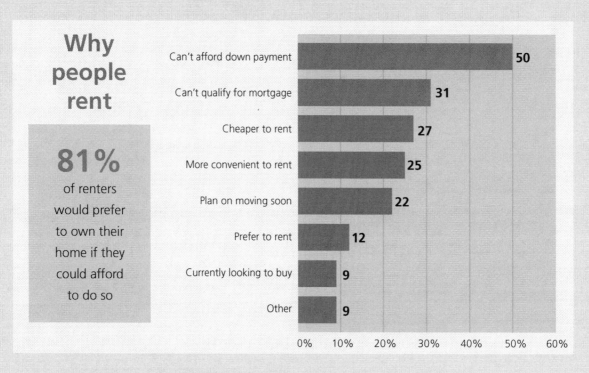

Why people rent

81% of renters would prefer to own their home if they could afford to do so

Can't afford down payment	50
Can't qualify for mortgage	31
Cheaper to rent	27
More convenient to rent	25
Plan on moving soon	22
Prefer to rent	12
Currently looking to buy	9
Other	9

Source: *Report on the Economic Well-Being of U.S. Households in 2014*, May 2015 (available in the Community Development section of the Federal Reserve Board's website, www.federalreserve.gov).

The results of the Federal Reserve's research and policy analysis inform Federal Reserve policymaking in various ways. Tracking and studying emerging issues allows the Federal Reserve to evaluate the impact that financial services and market trends may have on consumers and communities. Results are often published and disseminated to inform and foster discussion among regulators, industry groups, consumer and community advocates, and academic and policy organizations.

The Federal Reserve has produced consumer- and community-focused research and analysis that looks at consumer and household issues broadly, as well as a number of specialized topics, including

- unemployment and workforce development,

- community investment and stabilization,

- household economics and decisionmaking,

- consumers' use of mobile devices to connect with financial services,

- financial decisionmaking by the older adult population, and

- economic and credit conditions in low- and moderate-income populations and neighborhoods.

For examples of the Federal Reserve's research on consumer topics, visit the Community Development section of the Federal Reserve Board's website at www.federalreserve.gov.

- -

Community Economic Development Activities

Because a strong economy and strong communities go hand-in-hand, community development staff at the Federal Reserve Board and at each of the Federal Reserve Banks work at the national, regional, and local levels to help promote economic growth and financial stability in communities across the country, particularly neighborhoods that are low- and moderate-income and traditionally underserved.

Federal Reserve community development (CD) staff engage in a wide variety of activities, focused on four topical areas:

- **Policy and practice:** Promoting the well-being of economically vulnerable communities by enhancing the scale, sustainability, and impact of the broader community development field.

- **People:** Helping to sustain and promote policies that improve the financial stability and economic mobility of lower-income communities and individuals.

Figure 7.4. Federal Reserve community development efforts engage at the national and local levels

The Federal Reserve has dedicated staff in each of its offices throughout the country who work collaboratively to engage stakeholders; to understand issues and challenges in low- and moderate-income communities; and to provide research, policy insights, and technical assistance to support community and economic development programs. Community development staff are located in each of the Reserve Banks and Branches.

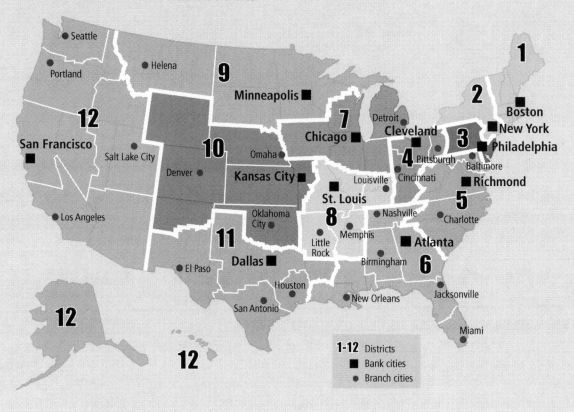

- **Place:** Engaging in "place-based" efforts to revitalize lower-income communities by advancing comprehensive community development efforts targeted to geographically defined areas.

- **Small business:** Working with intermediaries to support small businesses and microenterprises in order to help increase the capacity of funding and technical assistance providers; enhancing the availability of credit and capital for small businesses; and building a deeper understanding of small business trends and conditions.

The CD function of the Federal Reserve System is made up of dedicated community development departments at each of the 12 Federal Reserve Banks, as well as at the Board, that collaborate to advance effective community development policies and practices through a range of activities, including

- **Convening stakeholders:** The function brings together practitioners from financial institutions, nonprofits, governmental agencies, and the philanthropic and private sectors to collaborate on community and economic development initiatives and to identify both key challenges and promising practices to address them.

- **Conducting and sharing research:** The function provides policymakers and practitioners with objective analysis on the economic challenges facing lower-income communities and attendant policy and program implications. CD research is often posted online in blogs, articles, and working papers and is shared both in small group settings and at larger scale conferences.

- **Identifying emerging issues:** The function gathers and analyzes current information on economic and financial conditions to identify emerging issues affecting lower-income communities and individuals. For example, staff regularly conduct web-based polls or surveys of individuals and organizations to help track perceptions and provide market intelligence and sentiments around a wide range of CD issues.

The CD function supports the implementation of the Community Reinvestment Act through a wide range of activities, including assessing community economic development and credit needs, fostering conditions supportive of investment, lending and banking services in low- and moderate-income communities, and sharing information on lending and investment opportunities. CD also seeks to mobilize ideas, networks, and approaches that address a wide range of community and economic development challenges. The function leverages its capacity by working with intermediaries that offer financial, real estate development, advisory, and human services, rather than working directly with consumers or providing direct funding.

Working at the National Level

The community development program at the Board of Governors serves as the Federal Reserve's primary liaison to national community organizations and financial intermediaries on interagency projects and task forces. This effort convenes local and national stakeholders to discuss potential solutions to issues faced by communities throughout the country.

In 2015, the Board established its Community Advisory Council (CAC) to provide insights on the economic circumstances and financial services needs of consumers and communities, with a particular focus on the concerns of low- and moderate-income consumers and communities. The members of the CAC represent a diverse group of experts and representatives of consumer and community development organizations and interests, including from such fields as affordable housing, community and economic development, small business, and asset and wealth building. This council complements the Board's other advisory councils—the Community Depository Institutions Advisory Council and the Federal Advisory Council (see page 18 in section 2, "The Three Key System Entities," for more information on Board advisory councils).

In addition to the CAC, the Board seeks perspectives directly from community organizations, with community development staff collaborating with a wide range of private and public entities, such as Neighbor-Works America®, the Department of Housing and Urban Development, the Small Business Administration, the Department of the Treasury, the Department of Agriculture, and the Bureau of Indian Affairs.

The Board's community development staff also promote and coordinate systemwide, high-priority efforts. Initiatives have included close coordination with community development staff at the Federal Reserve Banks to study the impact of foreclosed properties on communities and consumers as well as the credit needs of small businesses. Such initiatives result in collaborations with a broad range of government agencies at the federal, state, and local levels, and conferences and other events

Promoting Consumer Protection and Community Development

Box 7.3. Community Development: Targeting the Challenges and Concerns on Main Street

The Federal Reserve leverages a network of regional Reserve Bank staff to support community development by targeting the specific, unique challenges faced by different communities throughout the country.

Community development website: The Federal Reserve's work in community development is captured in a central portal at https://fedcommunities.org. The site links the System's community development resources and research by topic and region.

Support for employment and workforce development: The Federal Reserve recognizes the challenges facing populations with historically higher unemployment rates, such as youth, the less-educated, and minorities, and works to help identify effective policies and practices that address obstacles to employment.

Support for small businesses and entrepreneurship: Viable small businesses and small-business owners are key to vibrant local economies. The Federal Reserve works to help identify opportunities to improve access to capital and credit for small-business development.

Support for neighborhood revitalization: The Federal Reserve supports efforts to align communities' development needs with available resources and advocates the strategic use of data and other tools to achieve this goal.

Federal Reserve staff and officials routinely convene conferences and events focused on community development issues. In April 2015, Chair Yellen gave opening remarks at the System's flagship biennial community development research conference, "Economic Mobility: Research and Ideas on Strengthening Families, Communities, and the Economy." (Conference materials are available at https://stlouisfed.org/community-development/economic-mobility-conference-2015.)

that brought together community organizations, lenders, academics, and government officials. These efforts also have resulted in publications and reports that share promising practices and policy solutions, as well as research and ongoing projects to address the challenges confronting lower-income communities and individuals.

Engaging at the Local Level

The community development issues faced by different regions of the
country are often unique to each region because of differing market
influences and trends. In recognition of this dynamic, the Reserve Banks
develop their own programs to target the most pressing community
and economic development needs and issues in their Districts.

Much of this work involves promoting mutually beneficial relationships
between local governments, financial institutions, nonprofit organizations, and the communities those entities serve. The Federal Reserve
Banks sponsor forums and conferences to provide research and policy
insights on community development issues and offer the opportunity
for stakeholders to engage face-to-face. In addition to bringing these
stakeholders together, community development staff provide them with
the information and technical assistance needed to develop and implement effective community and economic development programs.

Made in the USA
Coppell, TX
13 February 2022

73527001R00104